W9-DFG-375

GRAMMAR
Form and Function

3B

Milada Broukal

and

Ingrid Wisniewska, Contributing Author

McGraw-Hill

Grammar Form and Function 3B

Published by McGraw-Hill ESL/ELT, a business unit of The McGraw-Hill Companies, Inc., 1221 Avenue of the Americas, New York, NY 10020.

ISBN: 0-07-310410-8

Editorial director: Tina B. Carver
Senior managing editor: Erik Gundersen
Developmental editors: Arley Gray, Annie Sullivan
Editorial assistants: David Averbach, Kasey Williamson
Production manager: Juanita Thompson
Cover design: AcentoVisual
Interior design: AcentoVisual
Art: Eldon Doty

Photo credits:
All photos are courtesy of Getty Images Royalty-Free Collection with the exception of the following: *Page 14* © Reuters/CORBIS; *Page 95* © CP/JACQUES NADEAU; *Page 117* © Bettmann/CORBIS; *Page 118* © Michael Nicholson/CORBIS; *Page 147* © CORBIS; *Page 159* © Hulton-Deutsch Collection/CORBIS; *Page 171* © Helen Thayer; *Page 204* © Hulton-Deutsch Collection/CORBIS.

The *McGraw·Hill* Companies

Contents

UNIT 8 THE PASSIVE VOICE, CAUSATIVES, AND PHRASAL VERBS

UNIT 9 GERUNDS AND INFINITIVES

UNIT 10 AGREEMENT AND PARALLEL STRUCTURE

UNIT 11 NOUN CLAUSES AND REPORTED SPEECH

UNIT 12 ADJECTIVE CLAUSES

UNIT 13 ADVERB CLAUSES

UNIT 14 CONDITIONAL SENTENCES

APPENDICES

Acknowledgements

The publisher and author would like to thank the following individuals who reviewed *Grammar Form and Function* during the development of the series and whose comments and suggestions were invaluable in creating this project.

- Tony Albert, *Jewish Vocational Services, San Francisco, CA*
- Leslie A. Biaggi, *Miami–Dade Community College, Miami, FL*
- Gerry Boyd, *Northern Virginia Community College, VA*
- Marcia M. Captan, *Miami–Dade Community College, Miami, FL*
- Yongjae Paul Choe, *Dongguk University, Seoul, Korea*
- Sally Gearhart, *Santa Rosa Junior College, Santa Rosa, CA*
- Mary Gross, *Miramar College, San Diego, CA*
- Martin Guerin, *Miami–Dade Community College, Miami, FL*
- Patty Heiser, *University of Washington, Seattle, WA*
- Susan Kasten, *University of North Texas, Denton, TX*
- Sarah Kegley, *Georgia State University, Atlanta, GA*
- Kelly Kennedy-Isern, *Miami–Dade Community College, Miami, FL*
- Grace Low, *Germantown, TN*
- Irene Maksymjuk, *Boston University, Boston, MA*
- Christina Michaud, *Bunker Hill Community College, Boston, MA*
- Cristi Mitchell, *Miami–Dade Community College-Kendall Campus, Miami, FL*
- Carol Piñeiro, *Boston University, Boston, MA*
- Michelle Remaud, *Roxbury Community College, Boston, MA*
- Diana Renn, *Wentworth Institute of Technology, Boston, MA*
- Alice Savage, *North Harris College, Houston, TX*
- Karen Stanley, *Central Piedmont Community College, Charlotte, NC*
- Roberta Steinberg, *Mt. Ida College, Newton, MA*

The author would like to thank everyone at McGraw-Hill who participated in this project's development, especially Arley Gray, Erik Gundersen, Annie Sullivan, Jennifer Monaghan, David Averbach, Kasey Williamson, and Tina Carver.

Welcome to Grammar Form and Function!

In **Grammar Form and Function 3**, high-interest photos bring high intermediate to advanced grammar to life, providing visual contexts for learning and retaining new structures and vocabulary.

Welcome to **Grammar Form and Function 3**. This visual tour will provide you with an overview of the key features of a unit.

❖ **Form** presentations teach grammar structures through complete charts and high-interest, memorable photos that facilitate students' recall of grammar structures.

❖ **Form** presentations also include related information such as punctuation rules.

11b Noun Clauses Beginning with Wh- Words (Indirect Wh- Questions)

Form

I don't know **why he takes his computer on camping trips.**

Main Clause	Noun Clause (Indirect Question)*
She wanted to know	who I was.
	where they came from.
	why he called.
I don't know	when he arrives.
	what she said.
	how they did it so fast.

Indirect question is the name of this type of noun clause.

1. Noun clauses may also begin with wh- words. Sentences with noun clauses beginning with wh- words are also called indirect questions.

   Direct Question: Why did he call?
   Indirect Question: I don't know why he called.

2. Although wh- clauses begin with a question word, they do not follow question word order. Instead, they use statement word order.

   CORRECT: I know where **she is.**
   INCORRECT: I know where ~~is she.~~

3. We use a question mark at the end of a sentence if the main clause is a direct question and a period at the end of a sentence if the main clause is a statement.

	Main Clause	Noun Clause (Indirect Question)
Main clause is a question	Can you tell me	where the elevators are?
Main clause is a statement	I wonder	where the elevators are.

321
Noun Clauses and Reported Speech

Function

1. We usually use an indirect question to express something we do not know or to express uncertainty.

   I don't know **how much it is**.

2. We often use indirect questions to ask politely for information.

   Direct Question: What time does the train leave?
   Indirect Question: Can you tell me what time the train leaves?

---

4 | Practice

Rewrite each question as a main clause + a wh- noun clause. Be sure to use correct punctuation at the end of the sentences.

You are going to a job interview. What questions will you ask?

1. How many people does your company employ?

   Can you tell me _how many people the company employs?_

2. When did the company first get started?

   I'd like to know _____

3. Where is the head office?

   Can you tell me _____

4. What are the job benefits?

   Can you tell me _____

5. How many vacation days do people get?

   I wonder _____

6. What is the salary?

   Can you tell me _____

7. Who will my manager be?

   I'd like to know _____

8. When does the job start?

   Can you tell me _____

❖ *Extensive* **practice** guides students from accurate production to fluent use of the grammar.

❖ *Topical* **exercises** provide opportunities for students to use language naturally.

❖ *Your Turn* activities guide students to practice grammar in personally meaningful conversations.

9. How many people are you going to interview for this job?

   Can you tell me _____

10. When can you tell me the results of this interview?

    If you don't mind, I'd like to know _____

5 | Practice

Rewrite each direct question as an indirect question (a main clause + a wh- noun clause). Be sure to use correct punctuation at the end of the sentences.

You have a job interview tomorrow, and you are asking a friend to help you prepare. Your friend is telling you about the questions that they will probably ask you.

1. They will probably ask _what your current job title is._
   (What is your current job title?)

2. They will want to know _____
   (What are your job duties?)

3. They will ask _____
   (What qualifications do you have?)

4. They will want to know _____
   (Who was your previous employer?)

5. They will ask _____
   (How long did you work in your last job?)

6. They will want to know _____
   (Why did you leave your last job?)

7. They will ask _____
   (What was your salary?)

8. They will want to know _____
   (Why do you want the job?)

9. They will ask _____
   (How did you find out about the job?)

6 | Your Turn

Work with a partner. Think of an unusual job. Imagine that you went to a job interview for this job and write five wh- questions the interviewer asked you. Tell the class about the questions using a main clause + a wh- noun clause. Your classmates should guess the job.

Example:
(The unusual job was a lion tamer.)
They asked (me) why I was interested in lions.

1 Review

Rewrite the quotes and questions.

1. Cindy said, "Matthew, get out of bed, or you'll be late for your interview."

   Cindy told _Matthew to get out of bed or he'd be late for_

   his interview.

2. Matthew said, "Why didn't you get me up earlier?"

   Matthew wanted to know _____

3. Cindy said, "I was at the gym, and I expected you to be gone by now."

   Cindy said that _____

4. Matthew said, "Did I set my alarm clock or not?"

   Mathew couldn't remember _____

5. Cindy suggested, "Matthew, you'd better hurry if you want to get that job."

   Cindy suggested that _____

6. The interviewer had said, "Be here on time."

   The interviewer had insisted _____

7. Cindy said, "Why did you sleep so late?"

   Cindy said she didn't understand _____

8. Matthew explained, "I was preparing for the interview until 2:00 A.M."

   Matthew explained that _____

9. Cindy asked, "How do expect to get there, Matthew?"

   Cindy asked _____

10. Matthew asked, "Can you drive me there?"

    Matthew wondered if _____

11. Cindy asked, "How far is it to the office?"

    Cindy wanted to know _____

12. Matthew said, "It's about 20 miles."

    Matthew explained that _____

14. Susan warned, "We'll miss the bus."

    Susan warned Michael that _____

3 Review

Read the following fable from West Africa. Find and correct the errors in noun clauses and quoted and reported speech.

Ananse lived with his family. One year there was no rain, so the crops did not grow.
Ananse that knew ^ *that* there would not be enough food to feed everyone. One day his wife asked Will it rain at all this summer?

I don't believe so he replied. You know, I prefer to die than to see my children starve. Therefore, I will allow myself to die so there is enough food for the family. Ananse then told to his wife that he wants the family to bury me on the farm and to put into my coffin all the things I would need for my journey into the next world. He said, "It's critical that you left my grave open. I want my soul to be free to wander. And I insist that no one should visit the farm for three months after my death.

The next morning, Ananse's family found him dead. But Ananse was only pretending. At night he would lift the lid of his coffin and take food from the farm. One day his son, Ntikuma, realized that food was going scarce and that he must visit the farm to get some. He said he needed to go today to get what little food the farm had to feed the family. Where is all the corn and millet? he said to himself when he got to the farm. His mother told him the food was disappearing at night. It's a thief, exclaimed Ntikuma. I want to know who is he.

Ntikuma carved a statue from wood and covered it with tar*. Then he placed the figure in the field. That evening, Ananse came out of his coffin and saw the figure. Good evening he said. I don't know you. Please tell me who are you? The figure did not reply. Ananse got angry, so he slapped the figure. His hand stuck fast. Ananse shouted If you don't let go of his right hand, he'll hit you with his left! He hit the figure with his left hand. He hit with his right leg, then the left. Ananse struggled as the figure fell. He was stuck was very clear.

❖ *Review* Four review pages in each unit bring key grammar points together for consolidated practice and review.

❖ *Writing* assignments build composition skills such as narrating and describing through real-life step-by-step tasks.

WRITING: Write a Fable or a Legend

All cultures have stories. A fable is a story that teaches a lesson, which is called a "moral." The moral is usually stated at the end of the fable. In many fables, animals speak and act as humans do. A legend is a story, usually about famous people or events, that is handed down from generation to generation. It may be based in historical reality.

Step 1. Think of a legend or fable that you know. Tell it to your partner. Discuss its meaning to the culture it comes from.

Step 2. Write the events of your story in order.

Step 3. Write the story. Include quoted and reported speech from the characters. Write a title for your story. Here is an example of a fable.

The Fox and the Crow

One day a fox was walking through the forest when he noticed a crow up in a tree. The crow had a piece of cheese in its beak, and the fox was hungry. "That cheese looks delicious," the fox said to himself. He wondered how he could get the cheese. He thought, and he said,

---

SELF-TEST

A Choose the best answer, A, B, C, or D, to complete the sentence. Mark your answer by darkening the oval with the same letter.

1. I wondered where _____.

  A. he came from   Ⓐ Ⓑ Ⓒ Ⓓ
  B. did he come from
  C. came he from
  D. he did come from

2. My mother said, "Don't come in with your dirty shoes."
My mother warned me _____ in with my dirty shoes.

  A. to come   Ⓐ Ⓑ Ⓒ Ⓓ
  B. not come
  C. not came

6. "Don't drive too fast."

He told _____ drive fast.
  A. not to   Ⓐ Ⓑ Ⓒ Ⓓ
  B. to
  C. us not to
  D. to us not to

7. He asked, "Where do you want to go?"
He asked where _____.

  A. did I want to go   Ⓐ Ⓑ Ⓒ Ⓓ
  B. I want to go
  C. I wanted to go
  D. I want to go

❖ *Self-*tests at the end of each unit allow students to evaluate their mastery of the grammar while providing informal practice of standardized test taking.

B Find the underlined word or phrase, A, B, C, or D, that is incorrect. Mark your answer by darkening the oval with the same letter.

1. The teacher <u>warned</u> <u>us</u> <u>that</u> <u>not to</u> cheat
                 A   B   C   D
during the test.

                         Ⓐ Ⓑ Ⓒ Ⓓ

2. The interviewer <u>asked</u> <u>to me</u> when
                  A   B
<u>I wanted</u> to start <u>working</u>.
 C   D

                         Ⓐ Ⓑ Ⓒ Ⓓ

3. <u>Can you tell me</u> where <u>can I</u> get
      A   B
information about trains and where

6. Ted <u>said that</u> he <u>hadn't</u> <u>fill out</u> the
         A   B   C
application form <u>yet</u>.
              D

                         Ⓐ Ⓑ Ⓒ Ⓓ

7. <u>It is</u> <u>imperative that</u> <u>I fail not</u> any of
    A   B   C
my courses this year <u>if</u> I want to apply
                    D
to a university.

                         Ⓐ Ⓑ Ⓒ Ⓓ

8. Ted called from Boston yesterday and

To the Teacher

Grammar Form and Function is a three-level series designed to ensure students' success in learning grammar. The series features interesting photos to help students accurately recall grammar points, meaningful contexts, and a clear, easy-to-understand format that integrates practice of the rules of essential English grammar (form) with information about when to apply them and what they mean (function).

Features

* **Flexible approach to grammar instruction** integrates study of structures (form) with information on how to use them and what they mean (function).
* **High-interest photos** contextualize new grammar and vocabulary.
* **Comprehensive grammar coverage** targets all basic structures.
* **Extensive practice** ensures accurate production and fluent use of grammar.
* **Your Turn activities** guide students to practice grammar in personally meaningful conversations.
* **Review sections** bring key grammar points together for consolidated practice.
* **Writing assignments** build composition skills like narrating and describing through step-by-step tasks.
* **Self-Tests and Unit Quizzes** offer multiple assessment tools for student and teacher use, in print and Web formats.
* **Companion Website activities** develop real-world listening and reading skills.

Components

* **Student Book** has 14 units with abundant practice in both form and function of each grammar structure. Each unit also features communicative *Your Turn* activities, a *Review* section, a step-by-step *Writing* assignment, and a *Self-Test*.
* **Teacher's Manual** provides the following:
  * Teaching tips and techniques
  * Overview of each unit
  * Answer keys for the Student Book and Workbook
  * Expansion activities
  * Culture, usage, and vocabulary notes
  * Answers to frequently asked questions about the grammar structures
  * Unit quizzes in a standardized test format and answer keys for each unit.
* **Workbook** features additional exercises for each grammar structure, plus an extra student Self-Test at the end of each unit.
* **Website** provides further practice, as well as additional assessments.

Overview of the Series

Pedagogical Approach

What is *form*?

Form is the structure of a grammar point and what it looks like. Practice of the form builds students' accuracy and helps them recognize the grammar point in authentic situations, so they are better prepared to understand what they are reading or what other people are saying.

What is *function*?

Function is when and how we use a grammar point. Practice of the function builds students' fluency and helps them apply the grammar point in their real lives.

Why does **Grammar Form and Function** incorporate both form and function into its approach to teaching grammar?

Mastery of grammar relies on students knowing the rules of English (form) and correctly understanding how to apply them (function). Providing abundant practice in both form and function is key to student success.

How does **Grammar Form and Function** incorporate form and function into its approach to teaching grammar?

For each grammar point, the text follows a consistent format:

- ❖ **Presentation of Form.** The text presents the complete form, or formal rule, along with several examples for students to clearly see the model. There are also relevant photos to help illustrate the grammar point.
- ❖ **Presentation of Function.** The text explains the function of the grammar point, or how it is used, along with additional examples for reinforcement.
- ❖ **Practice.** Diverse exercises practice the form and function together. Practice moves logically from more controlled to less controlled activities.
- ❖ **Application.** Students apply the grammar point in open-ended communicative activities. **Your Turn** requires students to draw from and speak about personal experiences, and **Review** provides consolidated practice of key grammar points. **Writing** provides a variety of writing assignments that rely on communicative group and pair discussions, and **Expansion** activities in the Teacher's Manual provide additional creative, fun practice for students.

What is the purpose of the photos in the book?

Most people have a visual memory. When you see a photo aligned with a grammar point, the photo helps you remember and contextualize the grammar. The photo reinforces the learning and retention. If there were no visual image, you'd be more likely to forget the grammar point. For example, let's say you are learning the present progressive. You read the example "She is drinking a glass of water." At the same time, you are shown a photo of a girl drinking a glass of water. Later, you are more likely to recall the form of the present progressive because your mind has made a mental picture that helps you remember.

Practice

How were the grammar points selected?

We did a comprehensive review of courses at this level to ensure that all of the grammar points taught were included.

Does **Grammar Form and Function** have controlled or communicative practice?

It has both. Students practice each grammar point through controlled exercises and then move on to tackle open-ended communicative activities.

Do students have a chance to personalize the grammar?

Yes. There are opportunities to personalize the grammar in **Your Turn** and **Writing**. **Your Turn** requires students to draw from and speak about personal experiences, and **Writing** provides a variety of writing assignments that rely on communicative group and pair discussions.

Does **Grammar Form and Function** help students work toward fluency or accuracy?

Both. The exercises are purposefully designed to increase students' accuracy and enhance their fluency by practicing both form and function. Students' confidence in their accuracy helps boost their fluency.

Why does the text feature writing practice?

Grammar and writing are linked in a natural way. Specific grammar structures lend themselves to specific writing genres. In *Grammar Form and Function*, carefully devised practice helps students keep these structures in mind as they are writing.

In addition to the grammar charts, what other learning aids are in the book?

The book includes 38 pages of appendices that are designed to help the students as they complete the exercises. In addition to grammar resources such as lists of irregular verbs and spelling rules for endings, the appendices also feature useful and interesting information, including grammar terms, verb form charts, rules for capitalization and punctuation, and writing basics. In effect, the appendices constitute a handbook that students can use not only in grammar class, but in other classes as well.

Are there any additional practice opportunities?

Yes, there are additional exercises in the Workbook and on the Website. There are also **Expansion** activities in the Teacher's Manual that provide more open-ended (and fun!) practice for students.

Assessment

What is the role of student self-assessment in Grammar Form and Function?

Every opportunity for student self-assessment is valuable! *Grammar Form and Function* provides two Self-Tests for each unit – one at the end of each Student Book unit and another at the end of each Workbook unit. The Self-Tests build student confidence, encourage student independence as learners, and increase student competence in following standardized test formats. In addition, the Self-Tests serve as important tools for the teacher in measuring student mastery of grammar structures.

Does Grammar Form and Function offer students practice in standardized test formats?

Yes, the two Self-Tests and the Unit Quiz for each unit all utilize standardized test formats. Teachers may use the three tests in the way that best meets student, teacher, and institutional needs. For example, teachers may first assign the Self-Test in the Workbook as an untimed practice test to be taken at home. Then in the classroom, teachers may administer the Self-Test in the Student Book for a more realistic, but still informal, test-taking experience. Finally, teachers may administer the Unit Quiz from the Teacher's Manual as a more standardized timed test.

How long should each Self-Test or Unit Quiz take?

Since there is flexibility in implementing the Self-Tests and Unit Quizzes, there is also flexibility in the timing of the tests. When used for informal test-taking practice at home or in class, they may be administered as untimed tests. When administered as timed tests in class, they should take no more than 20 minutes.

How can I be sure students have mastered the grammar?

Grammar Form and Function provides a variety of tools to evaluate student mastery of the grammar. Traditional evaluation tools include the practice exercises, Self-Tests, and Unit Quizzes. To present a more complete picture of student mastery, the series also includes **Your Turn** activities and **Writing**, which illustrate how well students have internalized the grammar structures and are able to apply them in realistic tasks. Teachers can use these activities to monitor and assess students' ability to incorporate new grammatical structures into their spoken and written discourse.

Unit Format

What is the unit structure of **Grammar Form and Function**?

Consult the guide to *Grammar Form and Function* on pages X–XIII. This walk-through provides a visual tour of a Student Book unit.

How many hours of instruction are in **Grammar Form and Function 3?**

The key to *Grammar Form and Function* is flexibility! The grammar structures in the Student Book may be taught in order, or teachers may rearrange units into an order that best meets their students' needs. To shorten the number of hours of instruction, teachers may choose not to teach all of the grammar structures, or use all of the exercises provided. On the other hand, teachers may add additional hours by assigning exercises in the Workbook or on the Website. In addition, the Teacher's Manual provides teaching suggestions and expansion activities that would add extra hours of instruction.

Ancillary Components

What can I find in the Teacher's Manual?

* ❖ Teaching tips and techniques
* ❖ Overview of each unit
* ❖ Answer keys for the Student Book and Workbook
* ❖ Expansion activities
* ❖ Culture, usage, and vocabulary notes
* ❖ Answers to frequently asked questions about the grammar structures
* ❖ Unit quizzes in a standardized test format and quiz answer keys.

How do I supplement classroom instruction with the Workbook?

The Workbook exercises can be used to add instructional hours to the course, to provide homework practice, and to reinforce and refresh the skills of students who have mastered the grammar structures. It also provides additional standardized test-taking practice.

What can students find on the Website?

Students and teachers will find a wealth of engaging reading and listening activities on the *Grammar Form and Function* Website. As with the Workbook, the Website exercises can be used to add instructional hours to the course, to provide homework practice, and to reinforce and refresh the skills of students who have mastered the grammar structures.

UNIT 8

THE PASSIVE VOICE, CAUSATIVES, AND PHRASAL VERBS

8a The Passive Voice: Overview

Form

The Colosseum in Rome **was built** by the Romans. Competitions **were held** there. Today, some sports arenas **are named** after this building.

1. To form the passive voice, we change the object of an active voice sentence into the subject of a passive one. The subject of the active sentence can become the agent in a passive sentence. The agent tells who or what did the action in a passive sentence. It is introduced with the preposition *by*.

	Subject	Verb	Object
Active Voice	The pilot	**flew**	the airplane.
Passive Voice	The airplane	**was flown**	by the pilot.

2. We form the passive voice with a form of the verb *be* + a past participle. Questions use an auxiliary verb before the subject.

Subject	*Be*	(Other Auxiliary Verb)	Past Participle	
The Great Wall	**was**		**built**	by the Chinese.
The tourists	**are**	**being**	**shown**	around by the guides.

YES/NO QUESTIONS				
Auxiliary Verb	Subject	(Other Auxiliary Verb)	Past Participle	
Was	the Great Wall		**built**	by the Chinese?
Has	it	**been**	**visited**	by many people?

WH- QUESTIONS				
Wh- Word	Auxiliary Verb	Subject	(Other Auxiliary Verb)	Past Participle
When	**was**	the Great Wall		**built?**
How many people	**has**	it	**been**	**visited** by?

3. We form passive voice sentences with transitive verbs, which take objects. We cannot form passive voice sentences with intransitive verbs.

TRANSITIVE VERB	**fly**
Active Sentence:	The pilot **flew** the plane.
Passive Sentene:	The plane **was flown** by the pilot.

INTRANSITIVE VERB	**arrive**
CORRECT:	The plane arrived on time.
INCORRECT:	The plane ~~was arrived~~ on time.

Some common intransitive verbs are *appear, arrive, become, come, go, happen, occur, rain,* and *stay*. Motion verbs such as *go, come, walk, run,* and *arrive* are often intransitive.

Some transitive verbs do not have passive forms. These include stative verbs such as *cost, fit, have, resemble, suit,* and *weigh*.

CORRECT:	You resemble your father.
INCORRECT:	You ~~are resembled by your father~~.

Some verbs can be either transitive or intransitive. A good dictionary will tell you which verbs are transitive, intransitive, or both. Here are some examples.

Verb	Transitive Use	Intransitive Use
leave	She **left** her keys at home.	She **left** early.
move	I can't **move** that box.	Don't **move.** There's a snake next to your foot.
drive	I can **drive** a truck.	I'm tired. Would you **drive?**
play	We **play** soccer on weekends.	The children **play** nicely together.
work	Can you **work** this machine?	This computer won't **work.**

4. We use the passive voice in the following tenses. Note that the form of *be* is in the same tense as the tense of the active verb.

Tense	Active Voice	Passive Voice
Simple Present	He **washes** the car.	The car **is washed** by him.
Present Progressive	He **is washing** the car.	The car **is being washed** by him.
Present Perfect	He **has washed** the car.	The car **has been washed** by him.
Simple Past	He **washed** the car.	The car **was washed** by him.
Past Progressive	He **was washing** the car.	The car **was being washed** by him.
Past Perfect	He **had washed** the car.	The car **had been washed** by him.
Future with *Will*	He **will wash** the car.	The car **will be washed** by him.
Future with *Be Going To*	He **is going to wash** the car.	The car **is going to be washed** by him.
Future Perfect	He **will have washed** the car.	The car **will have been washed** by him.

We do not use the passive voice with some tenses because they sound awkward. These tenses are the present perfect progressive, the future progressive, the past perfect progressive, and the future perfect progressive.

5. Object pronouns (*me, him, her,* etc.) in the active voice become subject pronouns (*I, he, she,* etc.) in the passive voice.

ACTIVE SENTENCE			PASSIVE SENTENCE		
Subject	Verb	Object	Subject	Verb	
Thousands of people	elected	**her.**	**She**	was elected	(by thousands of people.)
The Chinese	built	**it.**	**It**	was built	(by the Chinese.)

Function

1. We use the passive voice when the agent (who or what does something) is not known or unimportant.

   The Great Wall **was built** hundreds of years ago. (The people who built the wall are not important to the meaning of the sentence.)

2. When we use *by* + an agent, it is usually because the subject of the sentence is more important than the agent, but we want to express them both.

   The economy was hurt **by last year's bad weather.**

We do not use *by* + an agent when the agent is a pronoun such as *you* or *they* used with a general meaning.

> Active Sentence: In this school, you obey the rules. (*you* = people in general)
> Passive Sentence: In this school, the rules are obeyed ~~by you~~.

Sometimes we do not use *by* + an agent because we do not want to mention the agent.

> Teacher: Some very basic grammar errors **were made** in last week's test.
> (The teacher doesn't want to say who made the errors.)

3. We often use the passive voice to make a sentence more impersonal, in situations involving rules, instructions, announcements, advertisements, or processes.

> Passengers **are requested** to show their passports along with their boarding passes.
> The time of the press conference **will be announced** later today.

4. We often use the passive when the agent is obvious from the meaning of the sentence.

> Olive oil **is used** a lot ~~by Italians~~ in Italy. (It is obvious that Italian people use it.)

---

1 Practice

Some of the following statements are true; some are false. If the statement is false, make it negative. Then follow it with a true statement using a word from the list. Use the present or past passive in your statement. If the statement is true, write "true" in the blank. Discuss your answers with a partner.

Alexander Graham Bell	Edmund Hillary and Tenzing Norgay
Brazil	earthquakes
calcium	Greece
discs	

1. Coffee is grown in Italy.

   Coffee is not grown in Italy.

   It is grown in Brazil.

2. The telephone was invented by Picasso.

   _____

   _____

3. Bill Gates started Microsoft.

_____

_____

4. The Taj Mahal in India was built by an emperor in memory of his wife.

_____

_____

5. The summit of Mount Everest was reached by Marco Polo.

_____

_____

6. The world's first Olympic Games were held in France.

_____

_____

7. Blood pressure is measured on the Richter scale.

_____

_____

8. *Hamlet* was written by Shakespeare.

_____

_____

9. Sugar is needed for strong bones.

_____

_____

10. Data on a computer is stored on plates.

_____

_____

2 Practice

Rewrite the headlines as complete sentences. Use the present perfect or simple past passive. Make any other changes that are necessary. (Remember that headlines often omit articles and words like *people*.)

1. Movie Star Questioned in Murder Case

   A movie star has been questioned in a murder case. OR

   A movie star was questioned in a murder case.

2. Higher Wages Demanded by Teachers

   _____

3. Twelve Injured in Friday's Earthquake

   _____

4. Plane Captured by Hijackers

   _____

5. Airport Closed; All Flights Canceled (Write two sentences.)

   _____

   _____

6. Ten Hospitalized After Gas Explosion

   _____

3 Practice

Rewrite the following newspaper paragraphs in the passive voice where appropriate. State the agent if it is important to the story.

1.

   Snowstorms have cut off many towns in the north. Snow has blocked the main highway to the north. People are unable to clear the road because the snow is still coming down heavily.

   Many towns in the north have been cut off by snowstorms

   The main highway…

   _____

   _____

2.

Somebody has stolen a total of two million dollars from the National Bank in New York City. Medical emergency workers took two guards to the hospital. The police have arrested three men in connection with the robbery. They are questioning another man.

_____

_____

_____

_____

3.

The Coast Guard found two teenage boys in a small boat far offshore yesterday. The boys and the boat had been missing since last Friday. The two boys were alive but weak. They took the boys to the hospital. Doctors expect them to recover soon.

_____

_____

_____

_____

4.

The police are seeking* two men in connection with a robbery at a gas station. They held up the cashier, but they did not injure him. While they were stealing the money, one of the men tied up the cashier. The men escaped in a black truck which the police think they used in other robberies in the same area.

_____

_____

_____

_____

* _Seek_ means "look for." The past participle of _seek_ is _sought_.

| 4 | Your Turn |

Find or create yourself three newspaper headlines from the news this week. Ask the class to make full passive sentences from each of them. Discuss whether it is possible to write all headlines in the passive voice.

Example:

Local Student Chosen for Big Scholarship—A local student has been chosen for a big scholarship.

8b The Passive Voice of Modals and Modal Phrases

Certain animals should be protected.

1. To form the passive voice of a modal expressing the present or the future, we use a modal + *be* + a past participle.

Subject	Modal	*Be*	Past Participle	
The sign	can		seen	by everyone.
The report	may		finished	on Tuesday.
The car	could*		repaired	in two days.
The work	might		given	to us.
The garbage	should		thrown out.	
His decision	ought to	be	respected.	
The rules	must		obeyed.	
Claudia	has to		told	the truth.
The workers	had better		paid	this week.
We	are supposed to		informed	about the delay.
We	will		invited	to the reception.
The date	is going to		changed.	

Could can refer to the past, present, or future, depending on the context.

2. To form the passive voice of a perfect modal (modal + *have* + past participle), we use a modal + *have been* + a past participle.

Subject	Modal	*Have Been*	Past Participle	
The project	should		finished	this week.
The Great Wall	must		built	a long time ago.
We	ought to	have been	informed	of the change.
The house	had better		cleaned.	

3. To form the past passive of expressions with *be* or *have*, we use the past forms of those verbs.

Subject	*Be/Have* Expression	Past Participle	
The students	**had to be**	**told**	that the trip had been canceled.
The house	**was supposed to be**	**painted**	the next day.
The computers	**were going to be**	**repaired,**	but weren't.

Function

1. We use the passive of *will* or *going to* to talk about the future.

   A new drug **will be produced** soon.
   More tests **are going to be performed** soon.

2. We use *can* to talk about ability in the present and future. We use *could* to talk about ability in the past.

   Our lives **can be extended** by this drug.
   The computer **could be repaired**, but the monitor **couldn't**.

3. We use *may, might,* and *could* to talk about present or future possibility.

   The new drug **may be tested** on patients this year.
   The drug **could be sold** in pharmacies in a year or two.

4. We use *should, ought to, had better,* and *must* to express advice or necessity.

   It **should be sold** to anyone who wants it.
   It **must be regulated** by law.

5. We use perfect modals with *can, could, should, ought to, may, might, must,* and *had better* to refer to the past.

   They **should have been told** about the change in the schedule.
   This report **must have been written** by one of the best students.
   They **can't have been held up in traffic**. The roads are clear at this hour.

5 | Practice

Read about elephants in Sri Lanka. Use the words in parentheses and the passive modal to complete the sentences. Some sentences refer to the past; others refer to the present.

Elephants are very important in Sri Lanka. They are important culturally, as they often lead religious processions. They are also important economically, as they (can/use)

_____ *can be used* _____ to haul timber. There used to be tens of
<u>1</u>

thousands of wild elephants in Sri Lanka, but now there are only around 3,000.

Why did so many elephants disappear? Some of the working elephants

(may/mistreat) _____ when they got old or sick.
<u>2</u>

Some of the wild elephants (may/shoot) _____ by
<u>3</u>

villagers who were trying to protect their crops. Other elephants

(may/force) _____ to leave the forests as the
<u>4</u>

human population increased over the years.

What (can/do) _____ to help save them?
<u>5</u>

How (can/more elephants/save) _____?
<u>6</u>

Sri Lankan authorities have decided that in the future many elephants

(will/move) _____ to protected
<u>7</u>

areas so people and crops won't be hurt, and the elephants

(can/preserve) _____ in safety. Better conservation
<u>8</u>

programs (will/establish) _____. Wildlife experts say
<u>9</u>

that more (should/do) _____ in the past to protect
<u>10</u>

the elephant population. This gracious and majestic animal

(must/not/allow) _____ to die out.
<u>11</u>

6 Your Turn

Write a paragraph about an environmental problem in your community. State the problem and write three or four sentences about what can be done to help solve it. Use passive modals in your sentences.

Example:

   There are too many cars in the city where I live. Cars should be banned from downtown. Downtown should be reserved as a pedestrian area. Parking lots could be built near downtown, and people could be taken to the stores and businesses by train or bus.

8c The Passive Voice with *Get; Get* + Adjective

Form

They have to get washed soon.

1. We sometimes use *get* in place of *be* in passive voice sentences.

Subject	*Get*	Past Participle	
I	**got**	**hurt**	by the falling tree branch.
You	**get**	**frightened**	by thunderstorms.
She	**gets**	**bored**	by long movies.
We	**will get**	**paid**	early this month.
They	**might get**	**delayed**	by the snowstorm.

2. We can also use *get* + an adjective. We can use *get* in any tense.

Subject	Get	Adjective
I	**will get**	**angry** if I'm late.
You	**got**	**cold.**
He/She/It	**gets**	**full** after a big meal.
We	**are getting**	**hungry.**
They	**get**	**thirsty** after a run.

3. The past participles of many verbs can be adjectives. We can use them after *get*.

Subject	Get	Past Participle as Adjective	
I	**will get**	**tired**	before the day ends.
He	**gets**	**bored**	quickly.
You	**got**	**scared,**	didn't you?

Function

1. We often use *get* + a past participle or *get* + an adjective in conversation instead of *be* + a past participle or *be* + an adjective. We rarely use the passive voice or *get* + adjective in formal writing.

2. We use *get* to emphasize action or change. We often use *get* in this way to suggest that something happens accidentally, unexpectedly, or unfairly.

   The vase **got broken** when I bumped into the table. (accidentally)
   She got awarded a big prize. (unexpectedly)
   I got blamed for losing the money. (unfairly)

3. When we use *get* + a past participle or an adjective, *get* usually means *become*.

   I **got hungry** by 11:00 in the morning. (= I became hungry by 11:00 in the morning.)

4. In some expressions, *get* does not mean *become*.

   get washed (wash oneself)
   get dressed (dress oneself)
   get started (begin doing something; or begin a trip)

5. We usually use *get*, not *become*, before the words *engaged*, *married*, and *divorced*, in speech and in writing.

   They **got engaged** last month. (It is possible to say *became engaged*, but this is rather formal.)
   They **got married** at the end of the year. (We do not use *become* with *married*.)
   We **got divorced** in January. (We do not use *become* with *divorced*.)

7 Practice

A. Read about Princess Diana's life. Use _get_ + one of the words from the list to complete the missing information. Use the correct tense. (Use _involved_ twice.)

blamed	divorced	jealous
criticized	engaged	killed
depressed	involved	married

Princess Diana was born on July 1, 1961. Who could have known then how tragically

her life would end? It was in 1980, on a trip to visit the royal family at Balmoral Castle,

that she _____got involved_____ romantically with Prince Charles. Diana and
                    1

Charles _____ on July 29, 1981, and from that moment on,
                    2

Diana was followed everywhere by photographers and journalists. Diana and Charles

_____ in St. Paul's Cathedral in London. But after her marriage,
          3

Diana _____ about her life with Charles and the royal family. People
                4

said that Charles _____ because of Diana's popularity. She was
                        5

beautiful and glamorous, but she understood the lives of ordinary people. They had two

sons, but their marriage was not happy. They _____ on August 28th,
                                                        6

1996. Afterwards, Diana _____ in humanitarian causes,
                                7

helping people with AIDS, and campaigning against landmines. On September 6th, 1997,

Diana and her friend Dodi Al Fayed _____ in a car crash in Paris.
                                            8

The Queen wanted a private funeral. But the British public wanted a public funeral to

express their grief. The Queen _____ for not showing enough
                                        9

emotion about Diana's death. In the investigation, the driver of the car, Henri Paul,

_____ for causing the crash by driving when drunk.
          10

B. Work with a partner. Ask your partner questions about the facts in the story.

Example:
You: What happened in 1980?
Your partner: Diana got romantically involved with Prince Charles.

8 | Practice

A. Read the sentences about Janice. What kind of person is she? Write *B* for the sentences in which *get* means *become*. Write *O* for sentences with other meanings of *get*.

___O___   **1.** Janice gets up at 8:00 A.M.

___B___   **2.** If she doesn't sleep enough, she gets tired by the end of the day.

_____   **3.** She gets dressed before having her breakfast.

_____   **4.** She gets her briefcase ready the night before.

_____   **5.** She gets irritated when the bus is late.

_____   **6.** She always gets her work done by the end of the day.

_____   **7.** She doesn't like it when her boss gets angry.

_____   **8.** She gets bored if she is not busy.

_____   **9.** She would like to get another job next year.

_____   **10.** She likes to go home before it gets dark.

_____   **11.** She usually gets sleepy by 9:00 P.M.

B. Discuss Janice with a partner. Give a reason why each of these characteristics applies (or doesn't apply) to her.

1. Janice is (a) punctual (b) lazy (c) confident.

2. Janice is (a) efficient (b) hardworking (c) impatient.

3. Janice is (a) energetic (b) ambitious (c) nervous.

Your Turn

Ask a partner these questions. Do you have the same or different reactions?

Example:

You:	When do you get irritated?
Your partner:	When I get held up in traffic.
You:	I don't get irritated in traffic, but I do get irritated when I have to wait in line for a long time.

1. When do you get angry?
2. When do you get bored?
3. When do you get depressed?
4. When do you get irritated?
5. When do you get worried?

8d *It* + a Passive Voice Verb + a *That* Clause

Form / Function

It **is said that** chocolate is actually good for you.

1. We can use *it* + a passive voice verb + a *that* clause to avoid mentioning an agent. We use this structure with past participles such as *believed, confirmed, considered, estimated, feared, hoped, known, mentioned, reported, said,* and *thought.*

ACTIVE SENTENCE	PASSIVE SENTENCE		
	It	Passive Verb	*That* Clause
People say that he is a billionaire.	**It**	**is said**	**that** he is a billionaire.

2. We can also use the subject of the active *that* clause as the subject of the passive sentence.

ACTIVE SENTENCE	PASSIVE SENTENCE		
	Subject	Passive Verb	*To Be*
People say that he is a billionaire.	He	**is said**	**to be** a billionaire.

10 Practice

Rewrite the sentences using *It is . . . that . . .*

1. We believe that calcium builds strong bones and teeth.

   It is believed that calcium builds strong bones and teeth.

2. We know that fruits and vegetables are important for our health.

   _____

3. Many doctors think that some fruits and grains can help to prevent cancer.

   _____

4. People say that fruit improves your immune system.

   _____

5. We believe that nuts help to lower cholesterol.

   _____

6. Dentists know that eating too much sugar can be bad for our teeth.

   _____

11 Practice

Work with a partner or the class. Complete the following statements with a noun + a passive voice verb. Use the past participles of verbs like *think, say, expect, report, or consider* + the infinitive in parentheses.

1. (to be) *Nora Jones is thought to be* _____ the best singer of

   the decade.

2. (to taste) _____ delicious, but I

   have never eaten it/one/them.

3. (to win) _____ the World Cup

   this year.

4. (to have) _____ a financial

recovery this year.

5. (to be) _____ good for your health.

---

12 **Your Turn**

Say or write five sentences with *is said, is known, has been known, is reported,* etc.
Use the following topics or think of your own.

Example:
The Japanese are known to have a healthy diet.

1. the Japanese
2. hamburgers
3. computers
4. the United States
5. my country

8e Present and Past Participles Used as Adjectives

Form

Ted felt **frustrated**.

1. We can use present participles* and past participles as adjectives.

Base Verb	Present Participle as Adjective	Past Participle as Adjective
tire	My job is **tiring**.	I'm **tired**.
relax	We had a **relaxing** vacation.	We felt **relaxed**.
excite	The game was **exciting**.	Everyone was **excited**.
shock	The **shocking** news spread quickly.	**Shocked** citizens demonstrated in the streets.

Present and past participles used as adjectives generally describe feelings. The two forms have different meanings.

1. Present participial adjectives describe someone or something that causes a feeling.

   The game was **exciting** (to me).
   Ted is **boring** (to Sandra).

2. Past participial adjectives describe someone who experiences a feeling.

   I am **bored**. (by the movie).
   He is really **confused** (by the question).

3. Here are some common participles used as adjectives.

Present Participle	Past Participle
amazing	amazed
amusing	amused
boring	bored
confusing	confused
depressing	depressed
embarrassing	embarrassed
exhausting	exhausted
frightening	frightened
impressive	impressed
interesting	interested
relaxing	relaxed
shocking	shocked
surprising	surprised

Present participle is another term for verb + *-ing*.

13 Practice

Read the story about a terrifying experience. Underline the correct adjectives in each underlined pair.

I had a (terrified / <u>terrifying</u>) experience when I went to Michigan a few years ago.
1

I had been driving all day, and I was completely (exhausted / exhausting). I stopped at
2

the first hotel I could find. It was an old hotel near the center of a small town. The hotel

looked a little rundown, and its dark windows were quite (depressed / depressing), but I
3

was so (tired / tiring) that I couldn't drive any farther to look for a better place. The desk
4

clerk looked very (surprised / surprising) that I had stopped there. The hotel wasn't cheap,
5

and when I saw the room, it was a little (disappointed / disappointing). I didn't notice any
6

other guests around. I went to my room and tried to watch TV, but all the programs were

(bored / boring). So I decided to read for a while until I felt (relax / relaxing) enough to
7   **8**

fall asleep. Suddenly I heard a strange creaking noise outside my door. It was very dark.

I couldn't see anything through the window. I was really (frightened / frightening). I went
9

back to bed. Then I heard the sound again, so I leapt out of bed and opened the door.

There was nothing there at all, but I noticed the front of the door was covered in scratch

marks. I packed all my things and ran for my car. I have never been so (terrified / terrifying)
10

in all my life.

14 Your Turn

Work with a partner. Tell your partner about an experience you have had. It can be a terrifying experience, an amusing experience, or an interesting experience. Use some present or past participles in your description.

8f Causative Sentences with *Have, Get,* and *Make:* Active Voice

I **have** the optician **check** my eyes every year.

1. We can form causative sentences with *have, get,* and *make* as the main verb.

THE CAUSATIVE WITH *HAVE* AND *MAKE*

Subject	*Have/Make*	Object	Base Verb
We	**have**	**our son**	**do** the dishes.
She	**had**	**her assistant**	**copy** the report.
The boss	**is going to make**	**everyone**	**work** late.
Tom's mother	**can make**	**him**	**stay** home tonight.

THE CAUSATIVE WITH *GET*

Subject	*Get*	Object	*To* + Base Verb
Tom	**gets**	**his sister**	**to do** the dishes for him.
I	**got**	**my friend**	**to drive** me here.
We	**are going to get**	**the store**	**to give** us a refund.
The boss	**should get**	**the staff**	**to work** late tonight.

2. We use a base verb after *have* and *make,* but we use *to* + a base verb after *get.*
3. We can use any tense or modal that makes sense in causative sentences.

4. We use the normal rules to form negative statements, questions, and short answers with the causative.

Negative Statements	We **don't make** our son do the dishes. She **didn't have** her assistant copy the report. The boss **isn't going to make** everyone work late. Tom's mother **might not make** him stay home tonight. Tom **didn't get** his sister to do the dishes for him.	
Yes/No Questions and Answers	**Do** you **have** your son do the dishes? **Did** she **have** her assistant copy the report? **Is** the boss **going to make** everyone work late? **Can** Tom's mother **make** him stay home tonight? **Did** you **get** your friend to drive you here?	No, I **don't**. Yes, she **did**. No, he**'s not**. Yes, she **can**. Yes, I **did**.
Wh- Questions and Answers	Who **gets** his sister to do the dishes for him? Who **does** Tom **get** to do the dishes for him? What **does** Tom **get** his sister to do? Who **made** Tom do the dishes? What **did** she **have** her assistant copy? Where **did** they **have** the taxi take them? When **will** you **have** the students take the test? Why **did** you **make** the children go to bed?	Tom **does**. His sister. The dishes. His mother **did**. The report. To the train station. Tomorrow. Because they were tired.

Function

1. We use the causative to talk about something that we require or arrange for someone else to do.

   I **had** the stylist **cut** my hair really short. (It's the stylist's job to cut my hair. I told him to cut it really short.)

2. We use *have* in a causative sentence when we normally expect someone, like a salesperson in a store, to do something for us.

   He **had** the salesperson **show** him 12 pairs of shoes.
 My boss **has** us **prepare** a progress report every week.

3. We use *get* when there is some difficulty involved, or when we have to persuade someone to do what we want.

   It took a long time, but I finally **got** my boss to **let** me take a week off.
 The teenager **got** his parents to **let** him take the car, but they told him to be very careful.

4. We use *make* when one person has power and/or authority over another. The person who does the action does not want to do it.

> The children's mother **made** them go to bed. (The mother has authority and power.)
> The robber **made** the clerk give him the money. (The robber does not have authority but does have power.)

15 Practice

A famous film director, Robert Ebbits, is traveling to New York City. His personal assistant is giving the hotel instructions. Rewrite the sentences as causatives.

Assistant: Mr. Ebbits will be arriving at your hotel tomorrow, and I want to make sure that everything is arranged for him.

Hotel Receptionist: Yes, of course. What can I do for you?

1. He likes to wake up punctually at 6:00 A.M. (have/the front desk/call him)

   Please have the front desk call him at 6:00 A.M.

2. He likes to read three daily newspapers first thing in the morning. (have/bellhop/deliver)

   _____

3. He likes to have fresh fruit and coffee for breakfast at 7:00 A.M. (have/room service/bring)

   _____

4. He doesn't like fresh flowers in his room. (have/the florist/put)

   Don't _____

5. He needs three shirts to be washed every day. (have/the laundry/wash)

   _____

6. He needs a computer, an Internet connection, a fax machine, and a flat-screen TV installed in his room as soon as he checks in. (get/the technical staff/install)

   _____

7. He wants his shoes polished and left outside his door every morning. (have/the bellhop/polish)

   _____

8. He needs a limousine waiting for him in front of the hotel each day at 9:00 A.M. (get/a chauffeur/bring)

   _____

8g Causative Sentences with *Have* and *Get*: Passive Voice

Form

Mary is **getting** the house **cleaned** because her in-laws are coming tomorrow.

1. We can form passive causative sentences with *have* and *get,* but not with *make.*

Subject	*Have/Get*	Object	Past Participle	
I	**have**	**my hair**	**styled**	by Lorenzo.
We	**have had**	**our car**	**serviced**	twice this year.
She	**had**	**her winter coat**	**cleaned**	last week.
He	**is getting**	**his car**	**washed**	this afternoon.
You	**should get**	**your eyes**	**tested**	soon.

2. When we use *have* or *get* in a passive causative sentence, we do not use *to* with the past participle.

> CORRECT: He got his hair cut.
> INCORRECT: He got his hair ~~to~~ cut.

3. We can use the causative with modals and in all tenses.

4. We use the normal rules to form negative statements, questions, and short answers.

Negative Statements	I **don't have** my hair styled by Lorenzo. He **isn't getting** his car washed this afternoon.	
Yes/No Questions	**Did** she **have** her winter coat cleaned last week? **Should** I **get** my eyes tested?	Yes, she **did.** No, you **shouldn't.**
Wh- Questions	Who **had** the car serviced? What **did** John **have** serviced?	John **did.** The car.

1. We use the passive form of the causative when we want to stress what was done and not who did it. We do not use *by* + an agent when we don't know who did it, or when it is not important who did it.

> She **has** her hair **styled** every week.
> I **got** the refrigerator **fixed**.

2. We use a *by* + an agent when it is important to mention the person doing the service.

> She **has** her hair **styled** by Lorenzo. (The speaker wants to mention the agent, Lorenzo.)
> I must **get** my suit **cleaned** this week. (The speaker is not interested in mentioning the agent.)

3. We can use the causative with *have* when something unpleasant or unexpected happens to someone.

> We **had** our passports **stolen** when we went on vacation.

16 Practice

Write one sentence about what you can have done (or get done) at each of these places.

1. copy shop	3. garage	5. laundromat	7. optician's
2. dentist's office	4. hair salon	6. dry cleaner's	8. tailor's

1. *You can get copies made at a copy shop. You can also get them bound.*

2. _____

3. _____

4. _____

5. _____

6. _____

7. _____

8. _____

Your Turn

What things would you have someone do for you, or have done for you, if you were in these situations? Talk with a partner.

Example:
If I were in the hospital, I would have my husband bring me something to read, and I would have flowers delivered.

1. if you were staying in an expensive hotel
2. if you were the president of a huge company
3. if you were in the hospital with a broken leg

8h   Phrasal Verbs

They're **putting on** makeup.

1. Phrasal verbs are very common in English. A phrasal verb consists of a verb + a particle. A particle is an adverb such as *up, down, away, out*. A verb followed by a particle has a different meaning from the verb alone. Sometimes we can guess the meaning of a phrasal verb.

   We **stood up**. (We got on our feet from a seated position.)

2. Sometimes we cannot guess the meaning of a phrasal verb. In these cases, we have to learn the special meaning of the phrasal verb.

   I'll **look up** the word. (I'll find information about the word in a dictionary, thesaurus, etc.)

INTRANSITIVE PHRASAL VERBS

3. Some phrasal verbs are intransitive. They do not take objects.

Subject	Verb + Particle
My car	**broke down** last night.
They	**eat out** every Saturday night.

Here are some common intransitive phrasal verbs.

Phrasal Verb	Meaning	Phrasal Verb	Meaning
break out	happen suddenly and unexpectedly	go out	leave the house; not stay home
break down	stop working (as a machine)	grow up	become an adult
break up	separate	hang up	end a phone conversation
dress up	put on nice clothes	show up	appear; be present
eat out	eat in a restaurant	speak up	speak loud/louder
fall down	fall to the ground	stand up	arise from a sitting position
get up	arise from a bed or a chair	start over	begin again
give up	stop trying to do something	stay up	remain awake
go down/up	increase/decrease	take off	go up (as an airplane); suddenly succeed (as a business); leave (informal)
go on	continue	work out	exercise

Some of these phrasal verbs can take objects, but the meaning is different. Phrasal verbs, like other verbs, can have different meanings.

The plane **took off** on time. (intransitive.)
We **took off our coats** because it was too warm.
(transitive; *take off* = *remove a piece of clothing*.)

4. Some intransitive phrasal verbs can be followed by a prepositional phrase, but the meaning of the phrasal verb does not change.

Bob and June **broke up**.
June **broke up with** Bob.

I **get up** every time I hear a noise.
She **got up from** her chair when the visitor arrived.

The Passive Voice, Causatives, and Phrasal Verbs

TRANSITIVE PHRASAL VERBS

5. Most phrasal verbs are transitive. Transitive verbs take objects.

Phrasal Verb	**Object**
Take off	your shoes.

There are two kinds of transitive phrasal verbs: separable and inseparable. Separable phrasal verbs are very common. Inseparable phrasal verbs are less common.

6. With separable phrasal verbs, the particle can go before or after a noun object. But when the object is a pronoun, the particle always follows the object.

SEPARABLE PHRASAL VERBS					
	Subject	Verb	Particle	Object	Particle	
Noun Object	I	**take**	**out**	the garbage		every morning.
	I	**take**		the garbage	**out**	every morning.
Pronoun Object	I	**take**		it	**out**	every morning.

INCORRECT: I take ~~out it~~.

7. With inseparable phrasal verbs, the particle always goes before the object.

INSEPARABLE PHRASAL VERBS					
	Subject	Verb	Particle	Object	
Noun Object	She	**got**	**over**	**her cold**	quickly.
Pronoun Object	She	**got**	**over**	**it**	quickly.

INCORRECT: We ~~came an interesting museum across~~.
INCORRECT: She ~~got her cold over quickly~~.

Here are some common separable and inseparable phrasal verbs and their meanings. Some of these phrasal verbs have additional meanings. Check a dictionary for other meanings.

Separable Phrasal Verbs	Meaning	Separable Phrasal Verbs	Meaning
bring up	raise a child; state something/someone as a topic	put on	place a piece of clothing on your body
call off	cancel something	set up	arrange for something
call up	telephone someone	start over	start something again
do over	do something again	tear down	destroy something completely
drop off	leave someone/ something somewhere	think over	reflect on someone/something
give up	quit something	think up	invent something
go over	review something	turn down	lower the volume on something
leave out	omit someone/ something	turn up	increase the volume on something
pick up	meet someone and take him/her somewhere	use up	use something until there is no more
put back	place something in its original location	wake up	cause someone to stop sleeping
put off	postpone someone/ something	work out	solve something

Inseparable Phrasal Verbs	Meaning
call for	come get someone
check into	register at a hotel; inquire into something
come across	find or discover someone/something by chance
get over	recover from something
go over	review something
look after	take care of someone/something
look into	investigate something
put up with	tolerate someone/something
run into	meet someone by chance

18   Practice

Read Mr. Jackson's schedule. Then answer the questions. Use pronouns in your answers. Remember that the position of pronouns is different for separable and inseparable phrasal verbs.

From: Company Management Tour Services

To: Interglobal Corporation, Inc.

Re: Mr. Jackson's Schedule, April 16–18, 20XX

16 April

Pick up Mr. Jackson from the airport at 6:45 P.M.

Drop off Mr. Jackson at his hotel at 7:30 P.M.

Mr. Jackson will check into the hotel at 7:35 P.M.

Meet tour guide who will look after Mr. Jackson during his stay.

17 April

Tour guide will call for Mr. Jackson at 7:00 A.M.

Set up a meeting to discuss the contract with the president at 9:00 A.M.

If the president decides to call off the meeting, we will call up Mr. Jackson immediately.

Afternoon and evening free; guided tour of city.

18 April

Pick up Mr. Jackson from the hotel at 10:30 A.M.

Meeting with president to go over the contract from 11:00 to 12:30 P.M.

Drop off Mr. Jackson at the airport at 1:15 P.M.

1. What time will they pick up Mr. Jackson from the airport?

   They will pick him up at 6:45 P.M.

2. What time will they drop off Mr. Jackson at his hotel?

   _____

3. What time will Mr. Jackson check into his hotel?

   _____

4. Who will look after Mr. Jackson during his stay?

   _____

5. What time will the tour guide call for Mr. Jackson the next morning?

   _____

6. For what time will they set up a meeting with the president?

   _____

7. What will they do if the president decides to call off the meeting?

   _____

8. What time will they pick up Mr. Jackson from the hotel on the final day?

   _____

9. When will Mr. Jackson go over the contract with the president?

   _____

10. What time will they drop off Mr. Jackson at the airport?

   _____

A. Complete the sentences with particles from the list. Use *down* two times. Use *up* four times.

across	out
after	over
down	up

I was born and brought ____up____ in Madrid. I was left alone a lot as a child and
                          1

learned to look _____ myself. I did a lot of reading. One winter, while I was
                2

getting _____ the flu, I came _____ a book about Sherlock Holmes, the
        3   **4**

famous fictional detective. I loved it! And that's when I started thinking _____
                                                                          5

mystery stories of my own and writing them _____. I designed elaborate covers for
                                           6

the books and used _____ all the paper in the house. I gave them as presents to
                   7

my family and challenged them to work _____ the solution to the crimes in my
                                      8

stories. My mother tried to get me to give _____ mystery stories and try some
                                           9

other form of fiction, but it was no good. Even now that I am older, I still read mysteries

in my spare time. There's nothing like a good mystery to calm you _____ after a
                                                                  10

hectic day.

B. Here is a list of synonyms for the phrasal verbs in part A. Write each phrasal verb next to the correct synonym.

1. find by accident   *come across*

2. invent   _____

3. make a note of   _____

4. quit   _____

5. raise   _____

6. recover from   _____

7. relax   _____

8. solve   _____

9. take care of   _____

10. use all of   _____

Take turns asking a partner these questions. Each one has a synonym for a phrasal verb in italics. In your answer, use a phrasal verb with a similar meaning as the italicized verb.

Example:

You: Where were you *raised*?
Your partner: I was *brought up* in Monterrey.

1. Where were you *raised*?

_____

2. Who *cared for* you when you were a child?

_____

3. Describe a day when you *found something by accident*.

_____

_____

4. Do you find it easy to *invent* excuses? Describe one time when you needed to invent and excuse.

_____

_____

_____

5. When do you usually *exercise*? What kind of exercise do you do?

_____

_____

6. How do you go about *solving* a problem?

_____

_____

_____

7. What kind of food or drink would you like to *quit*?

_____

8. What makes you *feel relaxed* after a hectic day?

_____

_____

Prepositions Following Verbs, Adjectives, and Nouns; Other Combinations with Prepositions

Form / Function

Alberto is **thinking about** something.

We use prepositions not only to show time, place, manner, and agent, but also in combination with verbs, adjectives, and nouns, and in many common expressions.

1. We use many verbs together with specific prepositions.

> You must **concentrate on** your work!
> I love to **listen to** the birds in the early morning.

Here are some common examples of verb and preposition combinations.*

Preposition	Examples			
about	think about	dream about		
at	laugh at	shout at	smile at	
for	account for	fight for	search for	wait for
from	come from	derive from	recover from	
in	believe in	delight in	result in	
of	think of	dream of		
on	concentrate on	depend on	plan on	rely on
	insist on			
to	belong to	contribute to	listen to	lead to
	speak to			

*Some verbs can take more than one preposition. For example, if you think **about** something, you consider it. If you think **of** something, it comes to your mind.

I **thought about** the problem all night.
I **thought of** a great place to go on Saturday night.

2. We use many adjectives with specific prepositions.

Are you **worried about** the test?
We are very **proud of** her.

Preposition	Examples			
about	angry about	excited about	worried about	
at	bad at	expert at	good at	surprised at (also *by*)
for	responsible for			
from	free from			
in	interested in	successful in (also *at*)		
of	afraid of	aware of	envious of	fond of
	proud of	tired of	typical of	
to	compared to	essential to	married to	opposed to
	related to	similar to		
with	bored with (also *by*)	disappointed with	pleased with	

3. We use many nouns with specific prepositions.

The **cost of food** has risen.
The senator didn't like the **results of the government's policies**.
I didn't know the **answer to her question**.

Preposition	Examples				
for	demand for	need for	reason for		
in	change in	decrease in	increase in	rise in	
of	cause of	cost of	danger of	evidence of	example of
	possibility of	result of	supply of	trace of	use of
on	impact on				
to	answer to	invitation to	reaction to	reply to	solution to
	threat to				

The Passive Voice, Causatives, and Phrasal Verbs

4. Here are some other common expressions that end in prepositions.

Preposition	Examples			
of	as a result of	because of	in spite of	in view of
	on account of	on behalf of	with the exception of	
to	according to	prior to		

5. There are also many common expressions that begin with prepositions.

Preposition	Examples			
at	at first	at last	at present	at the moment
	at times			
by	by accident	by chance	by land	by sea
	by air	by day	by night	
in	in common	in existence	in general	in the future
	in the past			
on	on fire	on land	on purpose	on the other hand
	on the whole			

21 Practice

Complete the sentences in each section with phrases from the list from that section.

A.
Nouns + Prepositions

an increase in   a threat to   one example of
an impact on   changes in

What is global warming? Global warming is ____*an increase in*____ the earth's
$\quad\quad\quad\quad\quad\quad\quad\quad\quad\quad\quad\quad$ 1

temperature, which in turn causes many _____ climate. These
$\quad\quad\quad\quad\quad\quad\quad\quad\quad\quad\quad\quad\quad\quad\quad\quad\quad\quad\quad$ 2

changes may have _____ plants, wildlife, and humans.
$\quad\quad\quad\quad\quad\quad\quad\quad\quad\quad\quad\quad$ 3

_____ a change caused by global warming is the rise in sea level,
$\quad\quad\quad\quad\quad\quad\quad$ 4

which may be _____ coastal communities and the people and
$\quad\quad\quad\quad\quad\quad\quad\quad\quad\quad\quad\quad$ 5

animals that live there.

B.
Adjectives + Prepositions

essential to   free of   opposed to   responsible for

What causes global warming? Most of the energy that is _____

the creation of the light and heat in our homes is produced by burning coal and gas, which

produces carbon dioxide. The carbon dioxide traps heat in the earth's atmosphere. Carbon

dioxide is _____ about half of our global warming. Many

environmentalists are _____ fossil fuels like coal and gas. They say

we should try to develop energy that is _____ pollution, such as

wave or wind energy. Then it will be possible to protect the climate as well as the animals

and people who live on the earth.

C.
Verbs + Prepositions

account for   contribute to   result in
come from   recover from

Another cause of global warming is a reduction in ozone in the outer layer of the

earth's atmosphere. Ozone is a gas that absorbs ultraviolet (UV) rays that

_____ the sun. Chlorofluorocarbons (CFCs) are chemicals that are

used in aerosols, air conditioners, refrigerators, and throwaway food containers. Scientists

believe that CFCs _____ the destruction of the ozone layer and

_____ a thinner layer of ozone in the outer atmosphere. As more of

the sun's ultraviolet rays enter our atmosphere, this _____ an

increase in cases of skin cancer. What can we do? Using CFC-free products is one way to

help our planet to _____ the damaging effects of ozone depletion.

---

22 | Your Turn

Talk with a partner about the causes and effects of global warming. Can you think of any solutions? Use some of the noun, verb, and adjective + preposition combinations from Practice 21.

REVIEW

1 Review (8a, 8e, 8i)

Underline the correct words.

Wouldn't you like to be able to (have / <u>get</u>) the weather to do what you want? Do you ever (get angry / have anger) because the weather is (depressing / depressed) and you want to have a (relaxing / relaxed) day at the beach? Well, you're not alone. Everyone would like their wishes to (be obeyed / obey). However, the weather (is obeying / obeys) no one. Everyone should delight (in / about) that fact because the weather has a big impact (on / for) our planet and is essential (on / to) our survival.

The sun (got worshipped / was worshipped) by ancient people. They believed (in / on) its importance to life on earth even though they didn't understand how it makes plants grow and how it affects the weather. The sun is (amazed / amazing). Our air, oceans, and land (are heated / heat) by the sun's energy. As the seasons change, the Earth (is / has) bathed in different amounts of energy from the sun. The result (for / of) this is a planet that has areas of hot and cold. The weather (gets / is getting) powered by these differences. Huge areas of hot and cold air (have / are) created by the heat and cold coming off water and land. These air masses must (have moved / move), or the cold areas (would get / are getting) colder, and the hot areas (would get / are getting) hotter. Fortunately, the earth keeps everything (on / in) balance by moving cold water and air from the poles toward the tropics, while warm water and air flow from the tropics toward the poles. As these areas of heat and cold move (around / over) and meet, wind, rain, and storms (are / have) produced. Crops grow, rivers run, and life on our planet goes (about / on).

Are you (having / going) to make the weather change? No, of course not. But (in / on) reality, you don't really want to.

2 Review (8a, 8b, 8d)

Read about Zanskar. Use the words in parentheses and the passive voice to complete the sentences. Some sentences require present tense verbs; others require past tense verbs.

High in India's western Himalayas, there is a kingdom called Zanskar. It (say)

is said/has been said that Zanskar is invisible because it (know)
   1

_____ by so few people in the outside world.
            2

For nine months every year, the Sensi-la Pass into Zanskar (block)

_____ by snow. In the winter, there is only one route that
            3

(can, take) _____ by travelers. It is a 112-mile journey through a
                        4

deep canyon on a frozen river. Traffic (can, carry) _____ on the river
                                                         5

for only a few short weeks each year before the ice starts to melt. It is a very dangerous

journey. Along the way, shelter (provide) _____ to travelers by caves
                                                    6

200 to 300 feet high on the canyon walls. Shelter (provide) _____
                                                                        7

by these caves for at least a thousand years. Because Zanskar is so remote, it has remained

independent for over 900 years. During this time, kingdoms around it (conquer)

_____ by outside armies many times.
            8

The little-known kingdom of Zanskar (rule) _____ by unknown
                                                        9

kings from 930 to 1836 C.E. Then it (take over) _____ by the Hindu
                                                            10

Dogras. In 1846, Zanskar (seized) _____ by the British, who never
                                          11

set foot on the land. Neither the Dogras nor the British ever took any interest in Zanskar.

In fact, Zanskar (ignore) _____ by most explorers until the
                                12

1820s, when the country (visit) _____ for the first time by a
                                    13

European. He was a Hungarian student named Alexander Csoma de Koros. Csoma de Koros

was no ordinary student. It (can, say) _____ that he performed one
                                            14

of the greatest achievements in travel for his day when he crossed Asia alone on foot.

In his travels, de Koros had met an English explorer named William Moorcroft who advised him to study the Tibetan language. After that, Csoma de Koros (introduce) _____ by Moorcroft to the King of Zanskar's secretary.
15
Csoma de Koros (invite) _____ to spend time at a Zanskar monastery.
16
He stayed there a year and returned one of Europe's first Tibetan scholars.

3 | Review (8f–8g)

Complete the sentences using *have, get,* or *make* and the verbs in parentheses in the active or passive voice. Use the correct tense.

1. Even though we're busy, I _____*got*_____ my boss (give) _____
   me the day off tomorrow.

2. When I was a child, I didn't like to do house work, but my mother _____
   me (clean) _____ my room before I could go out to play.

3. I _____ my computer (upgrade) _____ twice since I've
   owned it.

4. I _____ the painter (paint) _____ the room again after
   he painted it with the wrong color.

5. How does that teacher _____ her students (stay) _____
   so quiet?

6. My knee has been hurting for a week. I really have to _____ it
   (examine) _____ by a doctor.

7. My son's grades are too low. From now on, I _____ him
   (finish) _____ his homework before he goes out to play with his friends.

8. When will you _____ the students (take) _____ their
   examinations?

9. Who will John _____ (help) _____ him paint his apartment?

10. How can I _____ her (wear) _____ this dress if she
    doesn't want to?

4 Review (8h–8i)

Complete the sentences with phrases from the list.

demand for	pick up	tear up
dream of	solution to	trace of
impact on	take off	use up

At times, hikers _____*dream of*_____ getting extra help along the trail.* A day of
<u>1</u>

hiking with a backpack full of equipment can _____ a lot of energy.
<u>2</u>

Well, now there's a new _____ the problem. You can
<u>3</u>

_____ that heavy backpack and _____ your
<u>4</u> <u>5</u>

pace, because llamas are here to help. In South America, llamas have worked as pack

animals that carry heavy loads for 6,000 years. But now there's a new

_____ them among hikers throughout the U.S. and Canada. One of
<u>6</u>

the big advantages of using llamas is their low _____ the
<u>7</u>

environment. They don't _____ the trail like horses and mules.**
<u>8</u>

They leave barely a _____ their visit.
<u>9</u>

*trail: A path used for hiking, horseback riding, etc.
**mule: An animal that is a cross between a donkey and a horse

5 Review (8c, 8h)

Find the errors and correct them.

Melinda: Did you hear that Joe and Marian are ~~being~~ *getting* married?

Patrick: No way! They broke last month.

Melinda: They did, but I guess they decided to start out. Anyway, I don't know how she

puts with him.

Patrick: Him! You're not trying to have me believe that he's the problem, are you?

Melinda: No, you're right. Their problems must cause by both of them. I still can't believe

they're engaged. Do you think we can get them change their minds?

Patrick: I doubt it. Remember what write by Shakespeare: "Love is blind." Anyway,

don't be so worry. They'll work up their problems. They'll probably end over

being very happy.

WRITING: Write a Cover Letter

When you send an application form or a résumé to a company or a school, you send a cover letter with it. The purpose of a cover letter is to make the reader interested in reading your résumé or application.

Step 1. Pay attention to the format and organization of this letter.

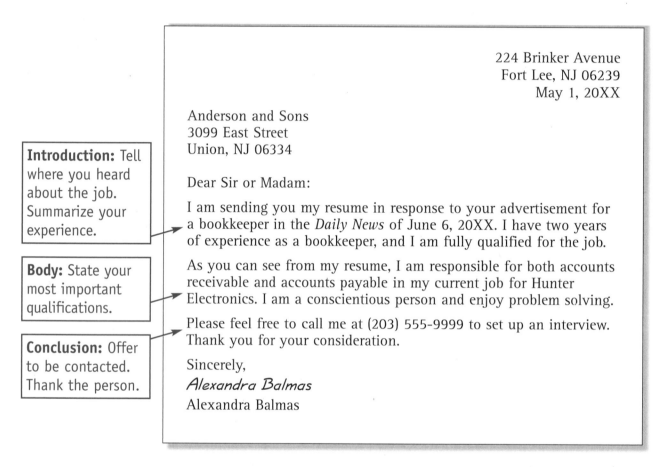

Introduction: Tell where you heard about the job. Summarize your experience.

Body: State your most important qualifications.

Conclusion: Offer to be contacted. Thank the person.

> 224 Brinker Avenue
> Fort Lee, NJ 06239
> May 1, 20XX
>
> Anderson and Sons
> 3099 East Street
> Union, NJ 06334
>
> Dear Sir or Madam:
>
> I am sending you my resume in response to your advertisement for a bookkeeper in the *Daily News* of June 6, 20XX. I have two years of experience as a bookkeeper, and I am fully qualified for the job.
>
> As you can see from my resume, I am responsible for both accounts receivable and accounts payable in my current job for Hunter Electronics. I am a conscientious person and enjoy problem solving.
>
> Please feel free to call me at (203) 555-9999 to set up an interview. Thank you for your consideration.
>
> Sincerely,
> *Alexandra Balmas*
> Alexandra Balmas

Step 2. Write a cover letter for a job that you would like to have. Type it on plain white paper (use a computer if possible). Send an original, not a photocopy.

Step 3. Evaluate your letter.

Checklist

_____ Did you use the format of the example letter?

_____ Did you follow the organizational model of the example letter?

_____ Do you think your letter would interest the reader? Would you get an interview?

Step 4. Work with a partner or a teacher to edit your letter. Check spelling, vocabulary, and grammar.

Step 5. Write your final copy.

A Choose the best answer, A, B, C, or D, to complete the sentence. Mark your answer by darkening the oval with the same letter.

1. You have to get a photo _____ for your passport.

   A. taking (A) (B) (C) (D)
   B. took
   C. taken
   D. to take

2. This is an example _____ a multiple-choice question.

   A. of (A) (B) (C) (D)
   B. in
   C. at
   D. to

3. I am going to the dentist next week to have _____.

   A. my teeth clean (A) (B) (C) (D)
   B. clean my teeth
   C. my teeth cleaned
   D. cleaning my teeth

4. The test results _____ next Monday.

   A. will have posted (A) (B) (C) (D)
   B. will posted
   C. will post
   D. will be posted

5. Hurry up and _____!

   A. get dress (A) (B) (C) (D)
   B. get dressed
   C. to get dressed
   D. getting dressed

6. _____ there was once water on the planet Mars.

   A. It is said that (A) (B) (C) (D)
   B. It is said to
   C. They say it was
   D. Says it

7. Ted is _____ about what to do.

   A. confuse (A) (B) (C) (D)
   B. confusing
   C. confused
   D. get confused

8. _____ the facts, we need more time.

   A. In view to (A) (B) (C) (D)
   B. In view of
   C. On view of
   D. By view of

9. I was late, so I _____.

   A. woke up him (A) (B) (C) (D)
   B. woke him up
   C. wake him
   D. him wake up

10. She's very _____ her job.

    A. a success in (A) (B) (C) (D)
    B. successful in
    C. successful for
    D. successful with

B **Find the underlined word or phrase, A, B, C, or D, that is incorrect. Mark your answer by darkening the oval with the same letter.**

1. Today's meeting <u>was postponed</u> <u>because of</u>
                 A   B

   a schedule conflict and a new time for the

   meeting <u>will been</u> <u>announced</u> later today.
           C   D

   Ⓐ Ⓑ Ⓒ Ⓓ

2. There has been an <u>increase in</u> demand for
                           A

   the buildings that <u>were built</u> in this area
                    B

   at the turn of the century; that is why

   they <u>are be</u> <u>renovated by</u> investors.
         C   D

   Ⓐ Ⓑ Ⓒ Ⓓ

3. Diamonds <u>are found in</u> different colors
             A   B

   and, <u>on general</u>, only shine when they
          C

   <u>are cut and polished</u>.
          D

   Ⓐ Ⓑ Ⓒ Ⓓ

4. A strange <u>coincidence</u> <u>was happened</u> when
             A   B

   the news <u>was</u> <u>announced</u> this
          C   D

   morning.

   Ⓐ Ⓑ Ⓒ Ⓓ

5. Some kinds of <u>fish cannot</u> <u>be ate</u>
               A   B

   <u>because of</u> contamination <u>from</u> industrial
     C   D

   waste.

   Ⓐ Ⓑ Ⓒ Ⓓ

6. In the past, <u>it was said</u> <u>that computers</u>
              A   B

   were too <u>complicating</u> for people to use
           C

   and <u>would be used</u> only for scientific
          D

   purposes.

   Ⓐ Ⓑ Ⓒ Ⓓ

7. <u>It is best</u> not <u>to leave out</u> multiple choice
     A   B

   questions on a test and <u>go them over</u>
                    C

   <u>at the end</u>.
      D

   Ⓐ Ⓑ Ⓒ Ⓓ

8. Everyone <u>was amazing</u> that
           A

   the painting <u>was stolen</u> with
             B

   <u>all the security precautions</u>
          C

   <u>were taken</u>.
      D

   Ⓐ Ⓑ Ⓒ Ⓓ

9. After the ancient artifacts <u>discovered</u>,
                     A

   construction on the site <u>was stopped</u>
                  B

   <u>by</u> the <u>city</u>.
    C   D

   Ⓐ Ⓑ Ⓒ Ⓓ

10. We <u>will have</u> <u>our computers service</u> next
        A   B

    week <u>by a company</u> that
          C

    <u>was recommended</u> by the bank.
       D

    Ⓐ Ⓑ Ⓒ Ⓓ

UNIT 9

GERUNDS AND INFINITIVES

9a Gerunds as Subjects and Objects; Verbs Followed by Gerunds

Daydreaming is useful.
Wanda **enjoys daydreaming.**

1. A gerund is a base verb + *-ing* that works like a noun. For example, a gerund can be a subject or an object in a sentence.

GERUND AS SUBJECT

Gerund Subject	Verb	
Painting	is	my favorite hobby.
Cycling	is	good exercise.
Scuba diving	takes	a lot of money.

GERUND AS OBJECT

Subject	Verb	Gerund Object
I	enjoy	**painting.**
He	stopped	**cycling.**

2. A gerund is always singular. When one gerund is the subject of a sentence, it takes a singular verb.

   Painting makes me happy.

   But if two gerunds form a subject, the verb is plural.

   Cycling and **diving are** my favorite sports.

3. Do not confuse a gerund with the present progressive.

   Cycling is a good sport. (*Cycling* is a gerund.)
   He **is cycling** in the park right now. (*Cycling* is part of the present progressive verb.)

1. We use a gerund as a noun.

   Painting is relaxing for me.

2. We can use a gerund after the following verbs and verb phrases.

admit	finish	quit
appreciate	give up	recall
avoid	imagine	resent
can't help	involve	resist
consider	keep/keep on	risk
continue	(not) mind	stand
delay	postpone	suggest
deny	practice	tolerate
discuss	prevent	understand
enjoy	put off	

   Have you **finished doing** your homework?
   I **enjoy walking** in the rain.

3. We usually use *go* + a gerund to describe recreational activities.

   We **went sightseeing** yesterday.
   Let's **go surfing**.

   Here are some expressions with *go* + a gerund.

go biking	go hiking	go shopping
go bowling	go hunting	go skating
go camping	go jogging	go skiing
go canoeing	go running	go swimming
go dancing	go sailing	go sightseeing
go fishing	go scuba diving	go surfing

1 Practice

Complete the sentences with the gerund form of verbs from the list.

camp	cycle	exercise	sail	sleep
climb	dive	jog	ski	swim

We are a very active family. In the winter, when there is snow, we pack up our skis and

go _____*skiing*_____ every weekend. In the summer, we take our tents and go
       1

_____ in the mountains. Our son Mark prefers mountain
        2

_____. We often go to the coast and do a lot of _____,
        3   **4**

_____, and _____. During the week, I take my running
        5   **6**

shoes to work so I can go _____ on my lunch break if the weather is good.
                                 7

And when my husband gets home from work, he takes his bike and goes

_____ for an hour or so. _____ regularly is very good for
        8   **9**

our health, and we're usually so tired at the end of the day that we don't have any

problems _____ at night.
              10

2 Practice

Rewrite the sentences using gerunds.

1. The doctor said I could get heart disease.

   The doctor said I risk _*getting heart disease*_____

2. "It might be a good idea to go on a diet," she said.

   She suggested _____

3. I decided not to drink coffee.

   I decide to give up _____

4. It's difficult not to drink coffee when I'm tired.

   It's difficult to avoid _____

5. I think that I shouldn't eat ice cream.

   I want to stop _____

6. I sometimes buy a small bag of potato chips. They are so good!

   Sometimes I can't resist _____

7. It's OK to count calories at every meal.

I don't mind _____

8. I used to cook a lot of rich food.

I used to enjoy _____

9. I have to learn to make new dishes with fewer calories.

I have to practice _____

10. I want to take care of my health.

I don't want to put off _____

3 │ Your Turn

Put the following list of activities in order from the most dangerous to the least dangerous, in your opinion. Then write a reason for each one of your choices. Discuss your opinions and reasons with a partner.

cycling   mountain climbing   skateboarding
hiking   scuba diving   swimming
jogging   skydiving

Activity	Reason
(Most dangerous) 1.	
2.	
3.	
4.	
5.	
6.	
7.	
8.	
(Least dangerous)	

Example:
You: I think that scuba diving is dangerous because there may be sharks in the water.
Your partner: I disagree. I don't think that sharks attack people very often.

9b Gerunds as Objects of Prepositions;
Gerunds after Certain Expressions

Form

Is he really interested **in studying** plant life in Antarctica?

1. Prepositions are words like *about, against, at, by, for, in, of, on, to, with,* and *without.* The noun or pronoun that comes after a preposition is the object of the preposition. A gerund works like a noun and therefore can also be the object of a preposition.

    She is interested **in him**.   (pronoun)
    She is interested **in seeing** him.   (gerund)

    Here are more examples of prepositions + gerunds.

	Preposition	Gerund	
What do you like	**about**	**living**	in a big city?
I am good	**at**	**learning**	languages.
He has plans	**for**	**decorating**	the house.
She stops him	**from**	**coming**	here.
He is interested	**in**	**working**	for us.
She is tired	**of**	**doing**	this job.
He insists	**on**	**checking**	my work.
They look forward	**to**	**seeing**	us tomorrow.
There's no point	**in**	**having**	a car in the city.

2. We use a gerund after many common expressions.

Expression	Example
Be busy	I'll **be busy doing** housework tomorrow.
Can't stand	He **can't stand waiting** in long lines.
Have difficulty/trouble	She **has difficulty learning** languages.
It's a waste of time/money	**It's a waste of time washing** the car because it's going to rain later.
*It's no use	**It's no use worrying** about it. There's nothing you can do.
It's not worth	**It's not worth waiting** in line for hours to see the game. We can see it on television.

*We can also say *there's no use (in) worrying about it.*

4 Practice

Jane has recently gone to an interview for a new job. Match the two halves of the interviewer's statements and questions.

___h___ **1.** Thank you

_____ **2.** We are excited

_____ **3.** We are thinking

_____ **4.** Are you interested

_____ **5.** Tell us about a time when you succeeded

_____ **6.** Are you capable

_____ **7.** Are you good

_____ **8.** What are your plans

_____ **9.** What would stop you

_____ **10.** We look forward

a. of taking on responsibility?

b. in solving a problem.

c. in working with databases?

d. about talking to you regarding this opportunity.

e. to seeing you again.

f. of hiring someone to manage our computer databases.

g. at dealing with stressful work situations?

h. for coming to this interview.

i. for developing your career?

j. from coming to work for us?

Read the numbered sentence in each of the following groups. Then circle the letter, a, b, c, or d, of the sentence with the same meaning.

1. I can't type your report because I'm too busy typing my own report.
   a. I can type my report but not yours.
   (b.) I can't type your report and mine, too.
   c. I'll type your report after I type mine.

2. It's not worth watching movies in the theater because they come out on DVD very quickly.
   a. The films are not good enough to watch in the theater.
   b. You might as well wait for the DVD to come out.
   c. Going to the cinema is too expensive.

3. There's no point in living in the city if you don't go out.
   a. If you don't go out, you don't benefit from living in the city.
   b. You don't have to go out if you live in the city.
   c. If you like to go out, you shouldn't live in the city.

4. It's a waste of time complaining about your cell phone service.
   a. If you don't complain, the service will be bad.
   b. If you complain, they will waste your time.
   c. The service will be bad whether you complain or not.

5. The exam is over. It's no use worrying about it now.
   a. Worrying about the exam will not help you now.
   b. You can't worry about the exam because it is over.
   c. You don't have to worry about the exam now that it's over.

6. I can't stand spending all of my money before the end of the month.
   a. I don't ever spend all of my money before the end of the month.
   b. Spending all of my money before the end of the month is OK with me.
   c. I really don't like spending all of my money before the end of the month.

---

6 Your Turn

Tell a partner two things that you are good at, interested in, and tired of.

Example:
I am good at drawing and playing basketball. I'm interested in movies and music.
I'm tired of eating the food here, and I'm tired of living in my apartment.

9c Verbs Followed by Infinitives

They **want to see** if they have passed the test.

1. We form an infinitive with *to* + a base verb. With some verbs, we use the verb + an infinitive.

Subject	Verb	Infinitive
We	agreed	**to look** after the children.
My parents	promised	**to visit** me this summer.
Everybody	wants	**to succeed**.

Here are some verbs that take infinitives.

afford	expect	need	refuse
agree	hope	plan	seem
appear	learn	pretend	threaten
decide	manage	promise	want

He can't **afford to buy** a computer.
She **threatened to resign** from the committee.

2. After some verbs, we can use the verb + an object + an infinitive.

Subject	Verb	Object	Infinitive
They	**encouraged** **asked** **persuaded**	**her**	**to stay**.

Here are some verbs that follow the pattern of verb + object + infinitive.

advise	invite	prefer	tell
allow	order	remind	warn
ask	permit	require	
encourage	persuade	teach	

3. With some verbs, we can use either of the structures in points 1 and 2 on page 263.

ask	help	want
expect	need	would like

The teacher **wants to leave** early. (The teacher will leave early if he can.)
The teacher **wants us to leave** early. (We will leave early because the teacher wants this.)

7 | Practice

Our neighbor, Rose, phoned us last night and this is what she said. Rewrite the sentences using the verbs in parentheses. Remember that some verbs need an object.

1. She said, "Please come to my house for a barbecue* with us on Saturday." (invite)

   She invited us to come to her house for a barbecue on Saturday.

2. She said, "Don't forget to bring the children." (remind)

   _____

3. She said, "Don't knock on the door loudly, or you'll wake up the baby." (warn)

   _____

4. She said, "Could you please bring a salad?" (would like)

   _____

5. She said, "I'm going to make a big chocolate cake. You'll love it." (promise)

   _____

6. She said, "Please come at 6:00 P.M." (want)

   _____

7. She said, "Try to be on time." (encourage)

   _____

8. She said, "You will be able to cook your own meat if you want." (allow)

   _____

9. She said, "You'll stay for a game of softball** too, won't you?" (expect)

_____

10. She said, "You don't know how to play softball? Don't worry. Just watch me play." (teach)

_____

*_Barbecue:_ An informal meal which is cooked and usually eaten outdoors
**_Softball:_ A game similar to baseball

8 | Your Turn

Choose one of the following questions. Discuss your answers with a partner.

Example:
My teacher expects me to do homework every night.
He wants me to watch English television for practice.
Sometimes he allows me to use a bilingual dictionary in class.

1. What things does your teacher expect, want, and allow you to do?

2. What do your parents expect, want, and allow you to do?

3. What does your boss expect, want, and allow you to do?

4. What does your husband/wife/friend expect, want, and allow you to do?

9d Verbs Followed by a Gerund or an Infinitive

Form / Function

She **loves to draw.**
She **loves drawing.**

Some verbs can take either an infinitive or a gerund. With some verbs, there is no difference in meaning, but with other verbs there is a difference in meaning.

1. These verbs can take either an infinitive or a gerund with no difference in meaning.

begin	hate	love
continue	like	start

It **started to snow**.
OR It **started snowing**.

2. With these verbs, there is a difference in meaning between the infinitive and gerund forms.

Verb	We Use Verb + Gerund:	We Use Verb + Infinitive:
forget	To say that we forget something after we have done it. I **forgot going** to their house. (I went there, but I forgot about it.)	To say that we forget something and don't do it. I **forgot to go to** the post office. (I was supposed to go there, but I didn't because I forgot.)
regret	To say that we regret something we have already done in the past. I **regret telling** him that I bought a car. (I told him I bought a car.)	To say that we regret something we have to do now. I **regret to tell** you that you have failed the test.*
remember	To say that we remember something after we have done it. I **remember going** to their house. (I went there, and I remember it.)	To say that we remember something before we do it. I **remembered to go** to the post office. (First I remembered, then I went there.)
stop	To say what we are doing before we stop. The class **stopped talking** when the teacher entered the room.	To say why we stop. The teacher **stopped to talk** to the principal when he entered the classroom.
try	To say that we intend to do an experiment to see what happens. I'll **try switching** the computer on and off to see if it will work.	To say that we intend to make an effort to see if we can do something. I **tried to fix** the computer, but I couldn't.

*Regret + infinitive is usually formal English.

9 Practice

Sherry is on the phone with her sister Susan. Read their conversation and underline the correct form in each underlined pair. Circle both forms if both are correct.

Susan: I've been thinking about our trip to Vermont last fall.

Sherry: Yeah. It was really great. Do you remember (to climb / <u>climbing</u>) up that steep
1

         mountain?

Susan: Yes. I'll never forget (to walk / walking) under all those red and gold leaves. I love
2

         (to hike / hiking) in the mountains.
3

Sherry: You know, I don't have copies of your photos. Please don't forget

         (to send / sending) them to me. Mine are terrible. I always try (to take / taking)
4   **5**

         them at special angles, but they never come out well.

Susan: Sure. I'm sorry that I forgot (to mail / mailing) them. Sherry, how about another trip
6

         next year? I was thinking that we could try (to go / going) on one of those organized
7

         tours. I know you hate (to travel / traveling) by bus, but it's really inexpensive.
8

Sherry: I know, but you don't have any freedom.

Susan: It's not that bad. They let you stop (to take / taking) photos along the way, and
9

         you get time on your own. I started (to look / looking) for some information on
10

         the Internet, but I got busy and couldn't finish.

Sherry: Well, we can check into them. You know, I can't stop (to think / thinking) about our
11

         Vermont trip. I agree that we should start (to plan / planning) another one soon.
12

10 Your Turn

Write a short paragraph that could be part of an e-mail message to a family member or a friend. Write three or four sentences and use at least three verbs from the list.

begin	enjoy	hate	remember	stop
continue	forget	love	start	try

Example:
     You know how much I love skiing. Did you know that I began to ski when I was only four years old? ...

9e Infinitives after Certain Adjectives, Nouns, and Indefinite Pronouns

She has a lot
of homework
to do.

1. We use infinitives after certain adjectives.

	Adjective	Infinitive	
It is	**important**	**to know**	a foreign language.
He was	**pleased**	**to see**	me.
We were	**disappointed**	**to hear**	the news.

Here are some adjectives that take infinitives.

afraid	determined	hesitant	proud
ashamed	eager	likely	ready
careful	happy	pleased	willing

2. We can use infinitives after nouns or after indefinite pronouns like *something* or *anything*.

	Noun/Pronoun	Infinitive
Do you have	**anything**	**to read**?
I have	**something**	**to eat.**
It's	**time**	**to leave.**
I have some	**letters**	**to write.**

1. The adjective in many adjective + infinitive combinations describes a feeling or attitude.

> She was **happy to hear** the news.
> We were **eager to try** the new restaurant.

2. When infinitives follow nouns, they often mean that there is an obligation or a necessity.

> I have some **letters to write**. (I must write some letters.)
> It's **time to leave**. (It's necessary for us to leave now.)

3. We use *for* + a noun or an indefinite pronoun when we need to say who does an action in the infinitive.

> It's convenient **for everyone** to have a computer in the classroom.
> I have some work **for James** to do.
> Do you have something **for me** to read?

II Practice

Complete the sentences with the infinitive form of the verbs from the list.

| aim for | do | finish | hear | think |
| be | find out | have | plan | travel |

Dear Henry,

I was very happy to _____*hear*_____ that you have decided to apply for
                            1

graduate school next year. As you know, your mother and I were very concerned

_____ that you were thinking of taking a year off. Of course, we'll
      2

support you, whatever you decide. But I'm sure you realize that it's very important for you

_____ your education. After you graduate from college, you'll have time
      3

_____ and do other things. But now it's good to have something
      4

_____. It's good for everyone _____ a goal in life. That
      5   6

has always been my philosophy. When you are young, it's easy _____
                                                                      7

that the future is not important. But believe me, and I know from experience, the

time _____ for the future is when you are young, not when it's too late
      8

_____ anything about it. Take my advice. Finish your education. It'll make
_____9_____

your mother and me so proud _____ there on your graduation day.
_____10_____

Love,
Dad

---

12 Your Turn

Complete the sentences. Explain your answers to a partner.

Example:
It's never too late to learn new things. For example, my grandmother has learned how to use a computer.

It's very important to . . .
It's never too late to . . .
There is never enough time to . . .
It's good to have something to . . .

9f   *Too* and *Enough* Followed by Infinitives

Form

She's **too** young to use a computer.
She isn't old **enough** to use a computer.

1. *Too* comes before an adjective or adverb. We use *for* + an object when we need to say who does the action in the infinitive.

Subject	Verb	*Too* + Adjective/Adverb	(*For* + Object)	Infinitive
It	is	**too cold**	(for the girls)	**to go** to the beach.
He	spoke	**too quickly**	(for me)	**to understand.**
It	isn't	**too late**	(for us)	**to go.**

2. *Enough* comes after an adjective or an adverb.

Subject	Verb	Adjective/Adverb + *Enough*	(*For* + Object)	Infinitive
It	isn't	**warm enough**	**(for the girls)**	**to go** to the beach.
He	spoke	**loudly enough**	**(for us)**	**to understand.**
She	is	**old enough**		**to go.**

3. *Enough* comes before a noun.

Subject	Verb	*Enough* + Noun	(*For* + Object)	Infinitive
There	isn't	**enough time**	**(for them)**	**to finish.**
We	have	**enough money**		**to buy** the CDs.

Function

1. When we use *too,* it has a negative meaning. It means that something is more than necessary or more than is wanted.

> She is **too** young to drive. (It is impossible for her to drive.)
> I'm **too** tired to go. (I cannot go.)

Do not confuse *too* with *very*. *Very* means to a great degree; to a great extent. It does not suggest more than necessary.

> I am **very** busy, but I can help you. (I am busy, but it is possible for me to help you.)
>
> I am **too** busy to help you. (I can't help you because I am busy.)

2. When we use *enough* in an affirmative sentence, it has a positive meaning. It implies that there is as much of something as is needed.

> She is **old enough** to drive.

But when we use *enough* in a negative sentence, it means that something is less than necessary or less than is wanted.

> This coffee is **not warm enough** to drink.

3. *Enough* usually comes before a noun. However, in formal English it occasionally follows a noun.

> INFORMAL: I have **enough** time.
> FORMAL: There is time **enough**.

Practice

Rewrite the sentences using *too* and *not . . . enough* and the words in parentheses.

Last week I went to a new restaurant with a friend. It was terrible!

1. The tea was so hot that we couldn't drink it.

   (hot/for us) *The tea was too hot for us to drink.*

   (cool/for us) *The tea wasn't cool enough for us to drink.*

2. The server spoke so fast that I couldn't understand her.

   (fast/for us) _____

   (slowly/for us) _____

3. The words on the menu were so difficult that I couldn't pronounce them.

   (difficult/for me) _____

   (easy/for me) _____

4. The room was so dark that I couldn't see the food.

   (dark/for me) _____

   (bright/for me) _____

5. The music was so loud that we couldn't have a conversation.

   (loud/for us) _____

   (quiet/for us) _____

6. I was so shy that I couldn't complain.

   (shy) _____

   (brave) _____

7. We were so disappointed that we didn't leave a tip.

   (disappointed) _____

   (satisfied) _____

8. We were so tired that we couldn't walk home.

   (tired) _____

   (energetic) _____

14

Your Turn

Tell a partner about yourself using *so* + adjective/adverb + *that*. Then ask your partner to tell the class about you using *too* or *not . . . enough*. Use the words in the list or your own ideas.

Example:
You: In the morning, I am usually so sleepy that I can't make breakfast.
So I usually eat at school.
When I was younger, I was so shy that I couldn't make many friends.
Now I'm more outgoing.
Your partner: My partner is usually too sleepy in the morning to make breakfast.
She eats at school instead.
Also, when she was younger, she wasn't outgoing enough to make many friends. She says she's more outgoing now.

ambitious	friendly	optimistic	sleepy
athletic	hungry	outgoing	thirsty
busy	lazy	pessimistic	
energetic	lucky	shy	

9g   The Infinitive of Purpose

Form / Function

We went to the jewelry store **to look** at rings.

1. We can use an infinitive to talk about the purpose of an action. This often explains why someone does something.

    I am saving **to buy** a new car.　　(My purpose in saving is to buy a new car.)
    I went to Miami **to see** Susan.　　(My purpose in going to Miami was to see Susan.)

2. We can also use *in order to* + a base verb instead of an infinitive to explain a purpose. This is usually more formal.

> I drank a lot of coffee **in order to stay** awake.
> We left early **in order to get** there on time.

3. In formal English, we use *in order not to* to express a negative purpose. In informal English, we usually use a clause with *so*.

> FORMAL: All employees should attend the meeting **in order not to** miss important news.
> INFORMAL: All employees should attend the meeting **so** they won't miss important news.

4. We can also use *for* + an object to show purpose.

> I went to the pharmacy **for** some medication.
> I went to the pharmacy **to buy** some medication.

---

15 │ Practice

Jan is planning a trip to Colorado. Write sentences using the infinitive of purpose to tell what she will need these items for. Use the phrases from the list.

boil water	find her way	keep mosquitoes away	sleep in
carry things	keep food cold	see in the dark	start a fire

1. matches *She needs matches to start a fire.* _____

2. a tent _____

3. insect repellent _____

4. an ice chest _____

5. a kettle _____

6. a flashlight _____

7. a backpack _____

8. a compass _____

Your Turn

What things do you need to buy or do before going on vacation? Where do you go to get them? Say or write sentences using *to* or *for*.

Example:
I usually go to the drugstore to get some air sickness pills and some sunscreen.
I sometimes go to the bookstore to look for guide books about the place I'm going.

9h Perfect Infinitives and Perfect Gerunds; Passive Voice of Infinitives and Gerunds

Form

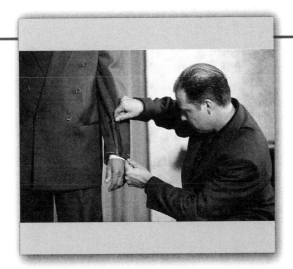

The sleeves **need to be shortened.**

ACTIVE FORMS OF INFINITIVES AND GERUNDS	
Form	Example
Simple Infinitive	Bob wanted **to do** the work by 5:00.
Simple Gerund	I enjoy **going** to parties.
Perfect Infinitive	Bob wanted **to have done** the work by 5:00, but he wasn't able to.
Perfect Gerund	I enjoyed **having gone** to Amy's party.

PASSIVE FORMS OF INFINITIVES AND GERUNDS*	
Form	Example
Simple Infinitive	She was lucky **to be awarded** the prize (by the judges).
Simple Gerund	I enjoy **being invited** to parties (by my friends).
Perfect Infinitive	She was lucky **to have been awarded** the prize (by the judges).
Perfect Gerund	I enjoyed **having been invited** (by Amy) to Amy's party.

*The agent may or may not be stated.

1. We use the perfect infinitive or perfect gerund to talk about something that happened at a time earlier than the main verb.

   My English seems **to have gotten** better. (My English got better before the time of speaking.)

   I remember **having met** her a year ago. (I met her before the time of speaking.)

2. We can also use the simple and perfect forms of infinitives and gerunds in the passive voice. The agent may or may not be mentioned. As in the active voice, we use the perfect form to talk about something that happened at a time earlier than the main verb.

   Thomas didn't expect **to be called** into the meeting (by his boss).   (simple infinitive)

   He was glad **to have been called** into the meeting (by his boss).   (perfect infinitive)

   Chloe dislikes **being given** extra work (by her boss).   (simple gerund)

   She disliked **having been given** extra work last week (by her boss).   (perfect gerund)

3. We can use simple and perfect gerunds as introductory phrases. See page 394 for more information on this kind of phrase.

   Before **deciding** on my destination, I talked to friends.
   Having decided to go on vacation, I called my travel agent.

4. We usually use an infinitive after the verb *need*.

   I **need to go** to the bank.

   But sometimes we use a gerund after *need*. In these cases, the gerund has a passive meaning. It usually shows that it is necessary to improve or fix something.

   My suit **needs cleaning**.
   His car **needs servicing**.

   We can also use a passive infinitive with the same meaning.

   My suit **needs to be cleaned**.
   His car **needs to be serviced**.

Complete the sentences with the simple or perfect form of infinitives or gerunds of the verbs in parentheses. Some answers must be in the active voice; others must be in the passive. Write one word on each line.

1. Kate was relieved (hear) __to__ __have__ __heard__ the news.

2. She was not really surprised (choose) _____ _____ _____ _____ as the best

   student by the class.

3. (receive) _____ _____ the highest score in every test, she was very happy.

4. She was pleased (be) _____ _____ so successful.

5. It had been hard for her (spend) _____ _____ _____ so much of her

   time studying.

6. She missed (not/see) _____ _____ _____ the latest movies.

7. (tell) _____ _____ _____ by her parents she would not get any more money,

   she had had no choice.

8. She also wanted (recognize) _____ _____ _____ as the intelligent child in her

   family instead of her brother!

Complete the sentences using the perfect gerund form of the verbs in parentheses. Some sentences require the active voice. The others require the passive.

Joe is writing an e-mail message to a new key pal. He is writing about his first job.

My first job was as a journalist for a local newspaper.

(spend) _____*Having spent*_____ four years in college earning a
                        1

degree in English, I thought I would be able to do the job easily. I was

pleased at (find) _____ the perfect job. After
                              2

(make) _____ many corrections on my first article,
                     3

my boss advised me to work harder. I tried hard, but I couldn't do better. After

(warn) _____ that I could lose my job, I started to worry.
                    4

I think most people would get worried after (tell) _____

5

that they would lose their job. I felt like a complete failure. I felt angry at

(treat) _____ unfairly. I told my uncle that after

6

(lose) _____ this job, I thought I would never find a job

7

again. (hear) _____ that, my uncle offered me a job

8

as his personal assistant working for his magazine!

19 Practice

**Rewrite the sentences using *need* + a gerund and *need* + a passive infinitive.
Use verbs from the list.**

clean	do	repair	sweep
cut	paint	replace	wash

We've just rented a house, but there are a lot of problems!

1. The windows are dirty.

    They need cleaning.

    They need to be cleaned.

2. The front gate is broken.

    _____

    _____

3. The grass is too long.

    _____

    _____

4. The floors are dusty.

    _____

    _____

5. The paint is coming off the walls.

    _____

    _____

6. The curtains are dirty.

_____

_____

7. The gas stove in the kitchen is old. We need a new one.

_____

_____

8. We have a lot of things to do!

_____

_____

20 Your Turn

What things need to be done in your house or apartment? Make a list and tell your partner about it.

Example:
My windows need to be cleaned.

9i Gerunds and Base Verbs with Verbs of Perception

Form

I **saw** a man **playing** music to a snake.

After some verbs of perception such as _see, hear, feel, smell, listen to, look at, notice, watch,_ and _observe,_ we can use an object + a verb + _-ing_ (present participle) or a base verb.

Subject	Verb	Object	Base Verb + -ing OR Base Verb
I	heard	Susan	**playing** the piano.
I	heard	Susan	**play** the piano.
We	saw	them	**leaving**.
We	saw	them	**leave**.

Function

There is usually little difference in meaning between the base verb + -ing and the base verb. However, in general, we use the base verb + -ing when we perceive (*hear, see, notice*) part of the action in progress.

I saw him **sleeping** in front of the television.

We use the base form when we perceive the whole action from beginning to end.

I saw him **sleep** through the whole movie from beginning to end.

21 Practice

Read the following questions. Is the question about a single complete action or an action in progress? Underline the correct form.

What would you do if . . . ?

1. . . . you saw someone (steal / stealing) your car?

2. . . . you saw someone (leave / leaving) their car lights on?

3. . . . you heard someone (break / breaking) into your house at night?

4. . . . you noticed some parents (shout / shouting) at their child?

5. . . . you heard someone (scream / screaming) and (fall / falling) down the stairs?

6. . . . you noticed a mouse (crawl / crawling) towards your chair?

7. . . . you saw a spider (sit / sitting) on your computer?

22 Your Turn

Say or write answers to the questions in Practice 21.

9j Person + Gerund

He insisted on **my leaving** the game.

1. In informal English, when we use a gerund to talk about what a person is doing, we usually use an object pronoun (*me, you, her, etc.*) + a gerund, or, if it is a person's name, the name (David) + a gerund.

    They insisted on **us going** with them.
    We were surprised at **David forgetting** to attend.

    In formal English, we usually use a possessive pronoun or noun.

    They insisted on **our going** with them.
    We were surprised at **David's forgetting** to attend.

2. In both informal and formal English, we use the object form after perception verbs such as *see, hear,* and *feel*.

    CORRECT: I saw him arriving.
    INCORRECT: I saw ~~his~~ arriving.

23 Practice

Rewrite the sentences with a person + a gerund. Give answers in both informal and formal English.

1. David forgot to call me on my birthday. I was surprised.

    I was surprised at David forgetting to call me on my birthday.

    I was surprised at David's forgetting to call me on my birthday.

2. He often phones me at work when I am busy. I don't like it.

_____

_____

3. He phones in the evening before 9:00. I don't mind.

_____

_____

4. He takes me dancing every Saturday night. My parents don't approve of it.

_____

_____

5. His friends talk on their cell phones all the time. I can't stand it.

_____

_____

6. I sometimes go out with other friends. He doesn't like me for it.

_____

_____

7. My parents tell me that David is not good enough for me. I don't listen to them.

_____

_____

8. My parents are always telling me what to do. I am tired of it.

_____

_____

24 Your Turn

Complete the sentences with true facts about yourself.

Example:
I can't stand people telling me what to do.

1. I can't stand people telling me _____.

2. I don't mind people telling me _____.

3. My friends criticize me for _____.

REVIEW

1 Review (9a–9d, 9f–9g, 9i)

Complete the sentences with a gerund or an infinitive.

Jack: I heard you went (camp)_____*camping*_____ over the weekend. I thought you
1

hated (do) _____ any outdoor activity.
2

Betty: I like (shop) _____ in flea markets, don't I?
3

Jack: Yes, (shop) _____ is your favorite pastime. But who persuaded
4

you (sleep) _____ under the stars?
5

Betty: You know I have trouble (say) _____ no. Anyway, I couldn't
6

avoid (go) _____. It was Stephanie's birthday. Besides, none of
7

us had enough money (stay) _____ in a hotel.
8

Jack: I see. Well, tell me all about it. I can't wait (hear) _____.
9

Betty: Do you really want to hear me (talk) _____ about it? It's a
10

very sad story. It all started at 5:00 Saturday morning. I was trying (get)

_____ some sleep when the phone rang. "It's time (get)
11

_____ up!" Stephanie said. Three hours later, we arrived at the
12

campground. We put up our tent, but I was still too sleepy (do)

_____ anything! I was also very upset because I'd forgotten
13

(bring) _____ my feather pillow. After the tent was up, we went
14

(hike) _____. At first, I refused (go) _____. But
15   16

I was too afraid (stay) _____ alone. We hiked and hiked. It was
17

awful. Terry warned me (stay) _____ on the path. But I saw
18

some wild flowers (grow) _____ in a field. I can't resist
19

(pick) _____ flowers. How did I know there was poison ivy*
20

there! Now I'm going crazy with all the (itch) _____. Not to
21

mention the insect bites. I had forgotten (bring) _____ my
22

insect spray. Finally, we got back to camp. All I thought about was

*poison ivy: a plant that irritates the skin and makes it itch

(eat) _____ dinner. But they said it was too early (eat)
    23

_____. They had (swim) _____ on their mind. By
    24   25

that time I was too tired (argue) _____. After they left, I
                                          26

thought I'd try (do) _____ some (cook) _____,
                          27   28

but there wasn't a stove. I tried (start) _____ a fire in the
                                                29

firepit. After an hour, I got a small stick of wood (light) _____.
                                                                  30

Then it started (rain) _____. There was no use even (think)
                              31

_____ about dinner. I decided I needed (go)
    32

_____ to bed. I had big plans for (sleep) _____.
    33   34

Then I discovered the leak in my tent.

2 Review (9b-9c, 9e, 9g–9h)

Complete the sentences with the correct gerund or infinitive form of verbs from the list.

be	do	rest	sleep	work
compete	meet	run	swim	worry
cycle	prepare	see	win	

I have always dreamed about ____competing____ in a triathlon. Tomorrow I'll see
                                        1

that dream come true. I'm nervous but, there's no use _____ about it. It's
                                                            2

more important for me _____ be part of this competition than
                              3

_____ it. I'm sure I'll have difficulty _____ tonight. But I'll
        4   5

have plenty of time _____ my sore muscles tomorrow night. I'm looking
                          6

forward to _____ all the other athletes at 5:00 in the morning. At 7:00,
                7

we'll start the triathlon by _____ in a lake for 2.4 miles. The next event
                                  8

requires us _____ over mountains and through deserts for 112 miles. Those
                  9

who are left can look forward to _____ 26.2 miles through the city streets.
                                        10

I insist on _____ this even though it's very difficult. _____
                11   12

very hard _____ for this event, I want _____ my dream
                13   14

come true.

3 Review (9c–9e, 9g, 9j)

Complete the sentences with the gerund or infinitive form of verbs from the list.

do	join	pay	snow
go	learn	read	think
hear	pack	remind	write

I'm so happy _____ that you're finally _____ on that
                        1   **2**

trip to Tibet. I've always wanted _____ something like that. I was thinking
                                                      3

about _____ you, but I'm saving my money _____ for my
                4   **5**

tuition next semester. Right now, it's more important for me _____ about
                                                                                            6

my future. I hope you don't mind my _____ you _____
                                                              7   **8**

some warm clothes. In those mountains, it can start _____ at any
                                                                              9

time of year. There are many great books about Tibet, so I hope you have done a lot

of _____. It's important _____ about a place before
           10   **11**

you visit. Well, have a wonderful time. Remember _____ me a letter!
                                                                        12

4 Review (9a–9e, 9g)

Complete the sentences with the correct gerund or infinitive verb form.

The appeal of (travel) ____*traveling*____ by bicycle is easy (understand)
                                        1

_____. It's healthy, good for (meet) _____ people, and
          2   **3**

anyone can do it. But (ride) _____ around a city park and (cycle)
                                          4

_____ around a country are two very different things. Before you take off
          5

on a bicycle tour, you need (be) _____ fit. Touring companies say that
                                                  6

before anyone starts (think) _____ about a cycling tour, they need (get)
                                          7

_____ in shape. They can do this by (start) _____ long
          8   **9**

before the trip starts. They urge people (get) _____ out and bike every
                                                                10

weekend in order (prepare) _____ themselves for 50-mile daily rides.
                                          11

Without some (train) _____, riders can count on plenty of sore muscles.
                                12

If you can't get outside (ride) _____ on the roads, then you must do some
                                              13

indoor exercise. You also need (do) _____ some (cross-train)
                                                    14

_____ In addition to (cycle) _____, you can do some
          15   **16**

Gerunds and Infinitives

(run) _____ 17, (hike) _____ 18 or even (swim)

_____ 19. (Get) _____ 20 ready for a bike trip, you should start

(build) _____ 21 your muscles four to six weeks ahead of time.

It's a good idea (know) _____ 22 what you can do before (commit)

_____ 23 yourself. "People need (have) _____ 24 some knowledge

of their abilities," says Dr. Ross of the Sports Institute. "Obviously, if someone can't go

up the stairs without (lose) _____ 25 their breath, they're not ready

(cycle) _____ 26 a couple of hundred miles."

If you are physically ready and like (cycle) _____ 27, you're going

(love) _____ 28 a cycle tour. There are tours all over the world, for all

levels, even beginners. So you don't have (be) _____ 29 a professional

(participate) _____ 30. There's nothing like (be) _____ 31

outdoors and (see) _____ 32 a country on a bicycle. It's like (have)

_____ 33 a great adventure. And there is something about (ride)

_____ 34 with other people that makes a trip more fun.

WRITING: Write an Essay of Analysis

An essay of analysis gives reasons or causes of something. See page 260 for general writing guidelines. See page 261 for information on writing an essay.

Step 1. Work with a partner or a group and analyze the topics. Make notes of the causes or reasons for each topic.

1. the causes of heart disease

2. the major causes of pollution in the world

3. how weather affects our lives

4. why marriage is good

Step 2. Choose one of the topics in Step 1, or think of your own.

Step 3. Write your essay.

1. Write a paragraph on each of the causes or reasons you have listed in your thesis statement. Make sure you have supporting examples and details for each.

2. Write an introduction to the topic. In your introduction, write a thesis statement: state your method of analysis (for example causes or reasons) and state your organizational method (for example, number of causes or reasons). Also summarize your key points. Here is an example of an introductory paragraph. The thesis statement is in bold.

> Preventing heart disease is a major public health effort in the United States. Some researchers say that heart disease appears to be on the decline, but we must persuade more people to pay attention to the risk that they face. One way to do this is by educating them about the causes of heart disease. **There are many causes of this deadly disease; however the three major causes are high blood pressure, genetic predisposition, and an unhealthy lifestyle.**

3. Write a conclusion. Restate your thesis statement and also state that there may be causes other than the ones you have listed.

4. Write a title for your essay.

Step 4. Evaluate your essay.

Checklist

_____ Did you write an introduction with a thesis statement?

_____ Did you write a paragraph about each of the points in the thesis statement?

_____ Are your reasons or causes clear? Do they support the thesis statement?

Step 5. Work with a partner or a teacher to edit your essay. Check spelling, vocabulary, and grammar.

Step 6. Write your final copy.

SELF-TEST

A Choose the best answer, A, B, C, or D, to complete the sentence. Mark your answer by darkening the oval with the same letter.

1. _____ a foreign language can sometimes be difficult.

   A. To learning   Ⓐ Ⓑ Ⓒ Ⓓ
   B. Learning
   C. Learn
   D. Be learning

2. I enjoyed _____ him write his essay.

   A. helping   Ⓐ Ⓑ Ⓒ Ⓓ
   B. to help
   C. help
   D. for to help

3. He _____ correcting my pronunciation.

   A. insist on   Ⓐ Ⓑ Ⓒ Ⓓ
   B. insist
   C. insists on
   D. insists to

4. We advised _____.

   A. to him not to go   Ⓐ Ⓑ Ⓒ Ⓓ
   B. him not go
   C. him not to go
   D. not him to go

5. On the way home, we stopped _____ some gas.

   A. getting   Ⓐ Ⓑ Ⓒ Ⓓ
   B. get
   C. to get
   D. for getting

6. We were eager _____ the new game.

   A. to try   Ⓐ Ⓑ Ⓒ Ⓓ
   B. trying
   C. try
   D. for to trying

7. We _____ to finish the test.

   Ⓐ Ⓑ Ⓒ Ⓓ

   A. didn't enough have time
   B. didn't have enough time
   C. had not time enough
   D. did not enough time have

8. The teacher saw _____ during the test.

   A. the student to cheat   Ⓐ Ⓑ Ⓒ Ⓓ
   B. cheat the student
   C. the student cheating
   D. cheating the student

9. He left a note for himself in order _____ forget.

   A. not   Ⓐ Ⓑ Ⓒ Ⓓ
   B. not for
   C. not to
   D. for not

10. We have an important issue _____.

   A. for discuss   Ⓐ Ⓑ Ⓒ Ⓓ
   B. for discussing
   C. to discussing
   D. to discuss

B **Find the underlined word or phrase, A, B, C, or D, that is incorrect. Mark your answer by darkening the oval with the same letter.**

1. <u>Drinking</u> <u>enough</u> water <u>is</u> important
   A   B   C
   <u>in order not get</u> dehydrated.
   D

   Ⓐ Ⓑ Ⓒ Ⓓ

2. After I <u>finished</u> <u>doing</u> my homework,
   A   B
   I <u>decided go</u> <u>for a walk</u>.
   C   D

   Ⓐ Ⓑ Ⓒ Ⓓ

3. The teacher was <u>pleased see</u> her students
   A
   <u>do well</u> on their final exam <u>before</u>
   B   C
   <u>graduating</u>.
   D

   Ⓐ Ⓑ Ⓒ Ⓓ

4. We <u>had been told</u> <u>by our teacher</u> not
   A   B
   <u>using</u> the internet <u>for</u> our research.
   C   D

   Ⓐ Ⓑ Ⓒ Ⓓ

5. After <u>having</u> a wonderful time
   A
   <u>hiking and seeing</u> friends at the camp,
   B
   I <u>look forward to</u> <u>go</u> there again
   C   D
   next year.

   Ⓐ Ⓑ Ⓒ Ⓓ

6. Meg: Could you help me with these
         math problems?

   Matt: Sorry. I don't have <u>time enough</u>
                              A
          <u>now</u>, but I <u>can help</u> you <u>later</u>.
          B   C   D

   Ⓐ Ⓑ Ⓒ Ⓓ

7. We <u>decided to go</u> on a trip to the
      A
   mountains but forgot <u>taking</u> the map, <u>so</u>
                         B   C
   we stopped <u>to buy</u> one at a gas station.
              D

   Ⓐ Ⓑ Ⓒ Ⓓ

8. <u>Watching bears</u> in the wild <u>are</u> <u>exciting</u>
   A   B   C
   and fun, but we must remember <u>to keep</u>
                                  D
   our distance.

   Ⓐ Ⓑ Ⓒ Ⓓ

9. <u>In order</u> <u>to be not</u> late for the flight and
   A   B
   have <u>enough time</u> for breakfast, I suggest
         C
   <u>getting up</u> at five in the morning.
   D

   Ⓐ Ⓑ Ⓒ Ⓓ

10. I always enjoy <u>to go</u> to the airport
                   A
    because it's nice <u>to sit</u> and watch the
                      B
    planes <u>taking off</u> and <u>landing</u>.
           C   D

    Ⓐ Ⓑ Ⓒ Ⓓ

UNIT 10

AGREEMENT AND PARALLEL STRUCTURE

10a Subject-Verb Agreement: General Rules Part 1

All the students in the photo **have** graduated.
Everyone is happy.

In an English sentence, the subject and the verb must agree in number. This means that a singular subject must have a singular verb, and a plural subject must have a plural verb.

Singular: John **is** a lawyer.
(*John* is a singular subject, and *is* is a singular form of the verb *be*.)
Plural: John and Alice **are** lawyers.
(*John and Alice* is a plural subject, and *are* is a plural form of the verb *be*.)

We form singular and plural forms of *be* differently from other verbs.

	Singular		Plural	
The verb *be* (present and past)	I	am/was	we	are/were
	you	are/were	you	
	he/she/it	is/was	they	
Other verbs in the present tense*	I	run	we	run
	you		you	
	he/she/it	runs	they	

*Note: *I* is a singular subject, and *you* can also be a singular subject, but they both take the base form of the verb. Only third person singular subjects (*he, she, it, Tom,* etc.) take the *-s* form.

Most of the time, subject-verb agreement is clear, but in some cases, even native speakers have to be careful. Here are some rules for special situations.

1. A sentence with two subjects joined by *and* takes a plural verb.

   The physics laboratory **and** the library **are** located on the first floor.

2. Some words like *mathematics* and *news* end in *-s,* but they are singular and take a singular verb.

> Mathematics **is** not my favorite subject.
> The news **is** good.

Other examples are *politics, physics, economics, aeronautics, electronics,* and *measles.*

3. When we use a gerund as the subject, it is always singular.

> Swimming **is** my favorite sport.

But if a subject has two gerunds, it is plural.

> Swimming and biking **are** my favorite sports.

4. When we use *each, every,* or *any* as an adjective in front of a subject, it takes a singular verb. This also includes indefinite pronouns like *everyone* and *everything.*

> Each of the subjects in a sentence **has** to agree with its verb.
> Everyone **wants** something from us.

5. When we use *all, almost all, most,* or *some* in front of a subject or as a subject, the subject takes a plural verb.

> **All** the students **eat** lunch at 12:00.   (*all* + a subject)
> **Most eat** in the cafeteria.   (*most* is the subject)
> **Some** of the students **eat** at home.   (*some* is the subject)

6. Two singular subjects joined by *or* take a singular verb. See page 307 for information on *either . . . or* and *neither . . . nor.*

> Thursday or Friday **is** the best day to go.

Two plural subjects joined by *or* take a plural verb.

> **Are** the boys or the girls going to leave first?

If one subject is singular and the other is plural, the verb agrees with the subject that is closest to it.

> I think that the potatoes or the chicken **is** burning.

> I think that the chicken or the potatoes **are** burning.

1 | Practice

Complete the sentences using the singular or plural form of the verbs in parentheses.

Every student whose first language is not English and who wants to go to college

in the United States (have) _____ *has* _____ to take an exam called TOEFL® (Test of

1

English as a Foreign Language). This exam tests your knowledge and skills in grammar,

vocabulary, reading, writing, and listening. Mathematics (be) _____

2

not included in the test. Reading (be) _____ the subject most students

3

have difficulty with. But listening and writing (be) _____ also difficult for

4

many students. Each student (apply) _____ to take the test individually.

5

The test can be taken on a computer or with pen and paper. Neither the handwritten test

nor the computerized test (be) _____ marked by a person. Everything,

6

except the essays, (be) _____ scored by computer. Each student

7

(receive) _____ a score by mail a few weeks later. Most colleges in the

8

country (require) _____ a certain score on this exam. Taking tests (be)

9

_____ a skill that requires a lot of practice.

10

2 | Your Turn

**What is the process of applying for college in your country? Write sentences
explaining what every student has to do, what most students have to do, etc.**

Example:
Every student has to write an essay.
Most students have to go to an interview.

10b Subject-Verb Agreement: General Rules Part 2

Here is your paper.
There are only two mistakes.
You got an A.

1. Prepositional phrases do not affect the verb. The verb always agrees with the subject.

   The value of his investments **is** dropping every day.

Subject	Prepositional Phrase	Verb	Complement
The value	of his investments	**is** dropping	every day.
One	of the students	**is**	here.
The directions	for operating this machine	**are**	confusing.

Phrases like *along with*, *together with*, *accompanied by*, *as well as*, and *in addition to* also do not affect the verb.

   The surgeon, together with his team of doctors, **is** visiting the patient.

   My parents, along with my brother, **are** going to visit me tomorrow.

2. When we begin a sentence with *here* or *there,* the verb may be singular or plural depending on the noun that follows.

   There **are** many students in class today.

   Here **is** the result of all your efforts.

3 | Practice

Complete the sentences with a singular or plural form of the verb *be*.

There _____*are*_____ twenty students in my daughter's class. Elena, along with
      1

all the other students, _____ taking a test right now. The subject of the
                 2

test _____ mathematics. All of the children _____
      3   4

allowed to use a calculator, which makes it easier. The instructions for the exam

_____ on the board. There _____ a separate answer sheet
      5   6

for each section of the exam. The answers _____ written in pencil. My
                                    7

daughter, along with all the other students in the class, _____ trying hard
                                                8

to pass the exam. All of the children, except Elena, _____ having trouble
                                        9

with the questions. Elena is one of the few students who _____ able to
                                        10

finish all the questions on time.

4 | Your Turn

**Describe the photo. What are all the
people doing? What are some of the
people doing? What is one person doing?**

_____

_____

_____

_____

_____

_____

_____

_____

_____

_____

_____

_____

10c Subject-Verb Agreement with Quantity Words

Three hundred dollars is enough.

1. We usually use a singular verb with expressions of time, money, distance, weight, and measurement. We do this because we think of the subject as a single unit.

   Ten dollars **is** all the money I have.
   Three miles **is** not far to run.
   Three weeks **is** a long time to wait for the results of the test.
   Twenty minutes **is** not enough time for an essay.
   Two cups of milk **is** what we need for this recipe.
   Two thirds of this box of cereal **has** been eaten.

2. We use the subject *the number of* + plural noun with a singular verb.

   The number of students in our class **is** twenty.

   We use the subject *a number of* + plural noun with a plural verb.

   A number of important people **are** here today.

3. When we use expressions of quantity such as *some of, a lot of,* and *three-quarters of* as the subject, the verb agrees with the pronoun or noun that follows *of*.

   Some of the orange **is** still good. (*some of the orange* = a part of the orange)
   Some of it **is** still good.
   Some of the oranges **are** still good.
   Some of them **are** still good.

However, we use a singular verb with these subjects: *one of the* + plural noun, *each of the* + plural noun, *every one of the* + plural noun, and *none of the* + plural noun.

> **One of the** students is sick.
> **Each of the** students is ready for the test.
> **Every one of the** students is on time for the test.
> **None of the** students **is** late.

In informal speech, we often use a plural verb with *none of the*.

> None of the students **are** late.

---

5 Practice

Look at the photo of the women having a friendly game of cards. Complete the sentences with the following quantity words.

a number of   each of the   none of the   one of the   the number of (use twice)

1. _____ *The number of* _____ women

    playing cards is four.

2. _____ women

    are sitting down at a table and playing cards.

3. _____ women

    is not holding a card.

4. _____ women

    is playing cards.

5. _____ are wearing jeans.

6. _____ cards on the table is unclear.

Make two sentences about the photo on your own.

7. _____

8. _____

6 | Practice

Read the sentences about the chart. Fill in the correct form of the verb in parentheses.

STUDENT SURVEY				
	Eat Dinner	Do Homework	Watch TV	Talk on the Phone
Student 1	20 minutes	60 minutes	90 minutes	45 minutes
Student 2	20 minutes	120 minutes	30 minutes	90 minutes
Student 3	20 minutes	60 minutes	90 minutes	15 minutes
Student 4	20 minutes	30 minutes	45 minutes	0 minutes
Student 5	60 minutes	90 minutes	120 minutes	30 minutes
Student 6	20 minutes	120 minutes	0 minutes	45 minutes
Student 7	60 minutes	60 minutes	30 minutes	20 minutes
Student 8	20 minutes	90 minutes	45 minutes	50 minutes
Student 9	20 minutes	60 minutes	60 minutes	120 minutes
Student 10	60 minutes	90 minutes	15 minutes	30 minutes
Student 11	60 minutes	30 minutes	45 minutes	45 minutes
Student 12	20 minutes	60 minutes	90 minutes	75 minutes
Student 13	20 minutes	120 minutes	120 minutes	15 minutes
Student 14	20 minutes	90 minutes	30 minutes	20 minutes
Student 15	20 minutes	30 minutes	90 minutes	0 minutes
Student 16	60 minutes	30 minutes	60 minutes	20 minutes
Student 17	20 minutes	90 minutes	120 minutes	0 minutes
Student 18	60 minutes	60 minutes	30 minutes	20 minutes

1. There (be) _____*are*_____ 18 students in this survey.

2. Two thirds of the students (spend) _____ twenty minutes eating dinner.

3. One third of the students (spend) _____ one hour on eating dinner.

4. None of the students (do) _____ homework for more than two hours.

5. All of the students (spend) _____ some time on homework.

6. One of the students never (watch) _____ TV.

7. Half of the class (watch) _____ TV for an hour or more.

8. Two thirds of the class (talk) _____ on the phone for less than an hour.

9. One sixth of the class (talk) _____ on the phone for more than an hour.

10. A number of students (not talk) _____ on the phone.

7 | What Do You Think?

1. Is forty minutes a long time to talk on the phone?
2. Is twenty minutes enough time to finish your homework?
3. Is more than one hour too much time to spend on eating dinner?
4. Is two hours enough time to spend watching TV?

8 | Your Turn

A. Interview six students in your class. Ask them how much of their time they spend on each of these activities every day.

Example:
You: How much time to you spend exercising every day?
Your classmate: I exercise for about an hour each day.

    exercising   eating   sleeping   watching TV

B. Tell the class about the results of your survey.

Example:
None of the students exercises for more than one hour a day.

C. Write a paragraph about the results of your survey.

_____

_____

_____

_____

_____

_____

_____

_____

_____

_____

_____

10d Parallel Structure

A good baseball player needs **stamina, concentration**, and **skill.**

1. We can use the conjunctions *and, but, or,* and *nor* to connect words or phrases. The words before and after these conjunctions must have the same grammatical form. When this is the case, there is parallel structure.

Grammatical Form	Example
Nouns	The essay had mistakes in **grammar** and **organization**.
Adjectives	His speech was neither **short** nor **good.**
Verbs	She **arrives** at seven and **leaves** at nine.
Adverbs	Does she work **slowly** or **quickly?**
Gerunds	**Dancing** and **watching** movies are my favorite weekend activities.
Infinitives	I like **to swim** but not **to fish.**

2. When a parallel structure has more than two parts, we use a comma to separate each part.

   The book contained **stories, poems,** and **plays.**
   His chores are **washing the dishes, cleaning the bathroom,** and **watering the flowers.**
   The instructor expects students **to attend** every class, **to do** all the assignments, and **to hand in** homework on time.

3. If a parallel structure has only two parts, we do not use a comma between them.

   I can speak Chinese and English.

9 Practice

Underline the parallel structure in the following sentences. Then write what grammatical form (nouns, adjectives, verbs, adverbs, gerunds, or infinitives) the parallel structure contains.

1. The colors you choose for your <u>clothes</u> and for your <u>home</u>, <u>office</u>, and <u>car</u> can have an effect on you. _____*nouns*_____

2. Colors have been known to ease stress, to fill you with energy, and even to reduce pain and other physical problems. _____

3. When you decide to paint your apartment, you shouldn't choose colors quickly or carelessly. _____

4. For example, the colors blue and green have a calming, relaxing, and peaceful effect.

   _____

5. On the other hand, the color red excites, stimulates, and warms the body.

   _____

6. The color yellow also energizes and stimulates the body, but not as much as the color red. _____

7. The color yellow is good for remembering things and relieving depression.

   _____

8. If you are sleeping and eating poorly, then orange is the color for you.

   _____

10 Practice

Underline and correct the errors in parallel structure in the sentences. Then write what grammatical form (nouns, adjectives, verbs, adverbs, gerunds, or infinitives) the parallel structure contains. Some sentences have no errors.

1. Blue makes people feel cooler in hot and <u>humidity</u> environments. _____*adjectives*_____
   humid

2. Try wearing black to feel strong and self-confidence. _____

3. Orange is the color for reducing fatigue and stimulate the appetite. _____

4. When you surround yourself with the color blue, you can help back problems, painful, and insomnia. _____

5. The color green helps people with emotional problems, heart problems, and cancer. _____

6. Yellow stimulates the mind, energizes the body, and creates a positive attitude. _____

7. The effect of color on our moods, healthy, and way of thinking has been studied for years. _____

11 Practice

Underline and correct the errors in parallel structure. Some sentences have no errors.

health
1. In order to maintain youth and good <u>healthy</u>, we need to have a combination of
nutrition
exercise and proper <u>nutritional</u>.

2. Exercise is good for our physical health and psychologically.

3. Regular exercise improves digestion, increases energy, burns fat, and lowering blood cholesterol.

4. It also reduces stress and anxious, which are the main reasons for many illness and conditions.

5. Also, regular exercise elevating mood, increases feelings of well-being, and reduces anxious and depression.

6. When you start an exercise program, remember to start out slowly, listen to your body, and gradually increase the strength and long of the exercise.

7. There are many different forms of moderate exercise including daily walking, bicycling, or even gardening.

12 Your Turn

Complete each sentence with your own words using parallel structure.

1. The night before a test, it is important to _____,

_____, and _____.

2. On the day of the test, you must be _____,

_____, and _____.

3. During the test, you must _____,

_____, and _____.

4. After the test, you can _____,

_____, and _____.

10e Coordinating Conjunctions

The ostrich is a bird, **yet** it doesn't fly.

1. We use a conjunction like *and, but, or, so, yet,* and *for* to connect two main clauses. We usually put a comma before the conjunction in a main clause.

   Susan has many problems, **but** she always looks happy.

   We can begin a sentence with *and* or *but*. Some instructors do not accept this usage. Check with your instructor.

   Susan has many problems. **But** she always looks happy.

2. We also use *so, for,* and *yet* to join two independent clauses. We usually use a comma before these conjunctions.

   I was very hungry, **so** I ate the whole cake.
   The actor doesn't appear in public, **for** he doesn't like publicity.
   He told me he would give back my money, **yet** he didn't.

   So, for, and *yet* also have other meanings.

   She is **so** smart. (adverb—*so = very*)
   I haven't finished **yet**. (adverb)
   I bought it **for** you. (preposition)

13 Practice

Punctuate the sentences with commas and periods. Use capital letters where necessary. Do not add other words.

Terry Fox was born in 1958 in Canada. ~~he~~ *He*

played soccer and basketball in high school for he loved sports

when he was eighteen he had problems with his knee so he went

to the doctor the doctor told him he had bone cancer and would

lose his leg this was a terrible shock yet Terry had an idea he

decided he could help people even with one leg his idea was to

run across Canada to collect money to fight cancer after the

operation he got an artificial leg and started to prepare for the

run his progress was very slow but he did not give up in 1980 he

started his run and called it the "Marathon of Hope" he ran 26

miles a day, seven days a week this was amazing but it was more

amazing because he had only one leg later that year Terry got sick again and had to stop

running he received letters from all over the world and Canadian television showed a

program about him the program collected $10 million for the Canadian Cancer Society

Terry Fox collected almost $24 million for cancer he died in 1981 but his story did not end

with his death Terry Fox events started all over the world and collected millions of dollars

to help fight cancer.

14 Practice

Punctuate the sentences with commas and periods. Use capital letters where necessary. Do not add other words.

A.

Dolphins live in the sea, yet they are

mammals. ~~they~~ *They* breathe air and give live birth

to their young young dolphins are intelligent

and sensitive animals their brains are almost

as large as ours and they have a language of

Agreement and Parallel Structure

more than 30 sounds for communicating with each other they live in groups of several hundred and always help any dolphins that may be in danger

dolphins are friendly to humans and there are many reports of dolphins helping people in danger in one case in 1983, a helicopter crashed into the Java Sea and it was a dolphin that saved the pilot's life the dolphin pushed the rubber raft for nine days until it reached the coast.

B.

Family names usually go from parents to children but some family names have the phrase "son of" to make the connection clear this happens in Scottish and Irish names, such as MacDonald or O'Connor *Mac* and *O'* mean "son of" so *MacDonald* means "son of Donald" and *O'Connor* means "son of Connor."

15	Your Turn

Write a paragraph describing your classroom. Use coordinating conjunctions and the correct punctuation.

Example:

Our classroom has a blackboard, desks, and chairs, but it doesn't have computers.

10f Correlative Conjunctions: *Both ... And;*
Not Only ... But Also; Either ... Or; Neither ... Nor

Form / Function

Malaika Mills is appearing **not only** in a movie **but also** in a play this year.

1. Correlative conjunctions come in two parts, for example, *both ... and*. We use these conjunctions to compare two ideas. We use the same grammatical form after each part of a correlative conjunction. Here are some examples of parallel structure with correlative conjunctions.

Parallel Structure	Example
both + verb + *and* + verb	Ben **both** studies **and** works.
not only + adjective + *but also* + adjective	Mary is **not only** generous **but also** intelligent.
either + noun + *or* + noun	I have to do **either** my homework **or** my chores.
neither + gerund + *nor* + gerund	He enjoys **neither** skiing **nor** hiking.

2. When we connect two subjects with *both ... and,* we use a plural verb.

   Both his brother **and** sister **are** in town.

3. When we connect two subjects with *not only ... but also, either ... or,* or *neither ... nor,* we use a singular or plural verb depending on the subject that is closest to the verb.

   Neither the doctor **nor** the nurse **is** with the patient.

   Neither the doctor **nor** the nurses **are** with the patient.

16 Practice

Circle the correct form of the verbs in parentheses.

1. Both vitamin C and calcium (is /(are)) important for good health.
2. Both your teeth and bones (need / needs) calcium.
3. Either milk or products from milk (contain / contains) a lot of calcium.
4. Both children and the elderly (require / requires) calcium.
5. Neither chicken nor pork (have / has) much calcium.
6. Not only milk products but also dark green vegetables (contain / contains) calcium.
7. Neither the liver nor the blood (make / makes) calcium.
8. Either food or drink (give / gives) the body the calcium it needs.

17 Practice

Combine the sentences into one with *both ... and, not only ... but also, either ... or* or *neither ... nor*.

1. Fruits have vitamin C. Vegetables have vitamin C.

   Both fruits and vegetables have vitamin C.

2. Heat destroys vitamin C. Exposure to air destroys vitamin C.

   _____

3. You can take vitamin C naturally in food. You can take vitamin C in tablet supplements.

   _____

4. Rice does not have vitamin C. Pasta does not have vitamin C.

   _____

5. Oranges have a lot of vitamin C. Lemons have a lot of vitamin C.

   _____

6. They say vitamin C prevents heart disease. They say vitamin C prevents colds.

   _____

7. Vitamin C does not prevent cancer. Vitamin C does not prevent infection.

   _____

8. Natural vitamins are good for the body. Synthetic vitamins are good for the body.

   _____

18 Your Turn

A. Complete the sentences about you and a partner in your own words.

Example:
Neither my partner nor I like baseball.

1. Neither my partner nor I _____

2. Not only I but also my partner _____

3. Both my partner and I _____

B. Report the information from part A to the class.

Example:
Both my partner and I like most sports, but neither of us likes tennis. My partner likes not only team sports but also individual sports such as running marathons.

C. Write a paragraph about what one of your classmates reported.

_____

_____

_____

_____

_____

_____

_____

_____

Agreement and Parallel Structure

REVIEW

1 | Review (10a–10c)

Underline the correct words.

Animals with a backbone (is / <u>are</u>) vertebrates. Scientists have recently discovered the earth's smallest vertebrate. It is the "stout infantfish."

When scientists first looked under the microscope, they instantly recognized it as something special. It is not only the world's smallest fish, but also (light / the lightest). This new species (are / is) no longer than the (wide / width) of a pencil. Both the male and the female (is / are) quite small. The female stout infantfish (measure / measures) a third of an inch. The male (is / are) just over one quarter of an inch. Each of these fish (weigh / weighs) very, very little. A load of 500,000 stout infantfish (weigh / weighs) barely one pound. Of course, no one (have / has) that many. As a matter of fact, there (is / are) only six specimens of this fish in laboratories today. The stout infantfish (are / is) very rare.

Neither the males (or / nor) the females (have / has) color, except for the eyes. Every one of these fish (lacks / lack) teeth, scales, and certain characteristics typical of other fish. Two months (is / are) not very long, but that (is / are) how long the stout infantfish live.

Everyone (want / wants) to know more about this tiny fish, but it is very hard to find them. Fishing (is / are) not the way to catch them, of course. The only ways (is / are) diving and (to explore / exploring) the deep ocean.

Scientists are very excited about the discovery of the world's smallest and lightest fish. Many (say / says) that discovering the stout infantfish (demonstrate / demonstrates) that scientists do not yet possess a complete list of marine (animal / animals). In fact, many important species (remain / remains) undiscovered.

2 | Review (10a–10b, 10d, 10f)

Underline the correct words.

The Maldives (<u>is</u> / are) an island republic located in the northern Indian Ocean. A
  1
chain of 1,190 islands (makes / make) up the Maldives. (All / Each) of the islands is a coral
  2 **3**
island. The 1,190 islands (is / are) organized into 26 groups called "atolls." The capital of
  4
the Maldives (is / are) Male. The climate (is / are) tropical. It (is / are) hot and
  5 **6** **7**
(humidity / humid). The weather throughout the islands (is / are) dry from November to
  8 **9**
March, but it is (rains / rainy) from June to August. November or January (is / are) the
  10 **11**
best month to visit the islands. The islands (is / are) small but (beautiful / beauty). There
  12 **13**
(is / are) many lovely beaches. Tourism (is / are) the largest industry. Fishing for the many
  14 **15**
species of fish in the warm waters (is / are) the second largest. The Maldivian people also
  16
(sells / sell) many of their beautiful crafts. Coconuts, sweet potatoes, and corn (is / are)
  17 **18**
their main agricultural products.

The Maldives (is / are) near the major sea routes in the Indian Ocean. Many ships on
  19
their way to Africa or Asia (has / have) crashed on Maldivian reefs. In 1602, a Frenchman
  20
named Francois Pyrard (hits / hit) a reef and (lost / loses) his ship. He swam slowly
  21 **22**
and (desperate / desperately) to shore. He could (neither / either) leave the island nor
  23 **24**
(rebuilding / rebuild) his ship right away. He decided to make the best of things by studying
  25
the culture, (learn / learning) the language, and later (write / writing) a book. The book
  26 **27**
(was / were) one of the most detailed books on early life in the Maldives.
  28

There (was / were) so many shipwrecks in the 1800s that the British ordered a survey
  29
of the islands so that the sailors would have accurate maps and (chart / charts). However,
  30
neither charts, maps, (or / nor) good sailing skill (was / were) of much help. The wrecks
  31 **32**
continued. To this day, it (is / are) still a dangerous area.
  33

Agreement and Parallel Structure

3 | Review (10a–10d)

Find the errors and correct them.

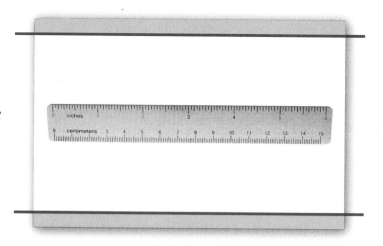

We measure things to find out how wide, ~~taller~~ *tall*, hot, cold, or ~~heavily~~ *heavy* they are. We needs accurate measurements in science and everyday activities such as cooking and when we sew. There is different types of instruments for measuring, and different instruments is used to measure long, wide, volume, mass, and temperature.

In the old days, people used objects along with their hands and feet for measuring. Having systems for measuring have always been important. Some cultures still uses ancient methods for measuring. One of these methods are the abacus. The abacus have been used in China since ancient times. With the abacus, you can add, subtraction, multiplying, and do division. Most people uses calculators to do that today. Each method have its own advantages.

There is many measuring tools. Every one of them are useful. We can measure long and width by using a ruler or a tape measure, and we measure weight by using a scale.

The metric system originated in France in 1795. It uses meters to measure length and grams for measuring weight. Most countries and scientists uses this system. The United States use the U.S. customary system. This system utilize feet and inches to measure length and pounds and ounces measures weight.

Two methods of measuring temperature is Fahrenheit and Celsius. Americans measures temperature by using the Fahrenheit scale. Fahrenheit register the freezing point of water as 32° and the boiling point as 212°. Most other countries uses Celsius. Celsius register the freezing point as 0° and the boiling point as 100°.

Which measuring systems do your country use?

Review (10a, 10c–10f)

Find the errors and correct them. Some of the errors are in punctuation.

Neil Armstrong and Buzz Aldrin walked on the moon on July 21, 1969. Neither
of them ~~are~~ *is* still there, of course, and one of their experiments are. Armstrong and Aldrin
wasn't only walking and jumped around on the moon. They was busy placing instruments
on the surface and conducted experiments. About an hour before the end of their final
moonwalk, they set up a science experiment, a two-foot wide panel with 100 mirrors. This
panel, along with many other objects, is still on the moon today, for no one have gone
back to get them. Neither the U.S. or any other country have gone back to the moon. The
exact number of objects on the moon are unknown. However, astronauts landing on the moon
today would find only one piece of equipment that are still working—the panel. None of the
other experiments are still running. The panel, called a "lunar laser ranging retroreflector
array," is small and simplicity, or it give scientists lots of important information.

The operation of the panel is simple. The mirrors on the panel points at Earth. A laser
pulse shoots out of a telescope on Earth, crossing the Earth-moon space, so hits the
mirrors. The mirrors sends the pulse straight back. On Earth, scientists measure the travel
time and determining the moon's distance, not only quickly but very accurate. For decades,
scientists, along with an occasional researcher, has traced the moon's orbit and learned
many remarkable things.

Everyone seem to have something to gain. The lunar laser ranging retroreflector array
have provided information to many fields of science. Physics are a good example. Physicists
has used the laser results to check Einstein's theories of gravity and relativity. So far,
Einstein are still considered correct, so who know whether the lunar laser ranging retroreflector array will someday tell us something different!

WRITING:

An essay of definition gives the writer's opinion of the meaning of a concept. See page 260 for general writing guidelines. See page 261 for information on writing an essay.

Step 1. Choose one of the terms below. With a partner or a group, brainstorm ideas about what these terms mean. Think of specific examples or situations that explain them.

1. friendship   **3.** a stranger

2. happiness   **4.** good parents

Step 2. Choose one of the terms above, or think of your own.

Step 3. Write your essay.

1. Write your body paragraphs. Each paragraph of your essay must illustrate a part of the definition stated in your thesis. Support each part with examples.

2. Write an introduction that defines the term you have chosen. You may define the term using a dictionary (name the dictionary and quote from it). In your thesis statement, tell how you are going to define it and give two or three aspects of the definition that you will write.

> Friends play a major role in a person's life. When you find a friend, your life changes. All of us have a different definition of what a friend is. According to the *American Heritage College Dictionary,* a friend is "a person whom one knows, likes, and trusts." For me, too, a friend is someone that I know, like and trust, but a friend is also someone with whom you share the same moral values, whom you support in times of need …

3. Write a conclusion that summarizes your definition. Give a final comment on the term.

4. Write a title.

Step 4. Evaluate your essay.

Checklist

_____ Did you write a thesis statement in your introduction?

_____ Did you give details, examples, or situations that support your thesis statement?

_____ Did you summarize and comment on your term in the conclusion?

Step 5. Work with a partner or a teacher to edit your essay. Check spelling, vocabulary, and grammar.

Step 6. Write your final copy.

SELF-TEST

A **Choose the best answer, A, B, C, or D, to complete the sentence. Mark your answer by darkening the oval with the same letter.**

1. Kate runs and _____.

   A. lifts weights   Ⓐ Ⓑ Ⓒ Ⓓ
   B. is lifting weights
   C. weight lifting
   D. is doing weight lifting

2. The doctor recommended eating healthier meals and _____.

   A. to do exercise   Ⓐ Ⓑ Ⓒ Ⓓ
   B. doing exercise
   C. exercise
   D. to exercise

3. The store sells not only vitamins _____.

   A. but also food   Ⓐ Ⓑ Ⓒ Ⓓ
   B. also sells food
   C. but sells food
   D. but also is selling food

4. Neither his grammar _____ good.

   Ⓐ Ⓑ Ⓒ Ⓓ
   A. or his reading skills are
   B. nor his reading skills is
   C. nor his reading skills are
   D. or his reading skills are not

5. He told me he would help me, _____ he didn't.

   A. so   Ⓐ Ⓑ Ⓒ Ⓓ
   B. for
   C. and
   D. yet

6. Both the students _____ at the meeting.

   Ⓐ Ⓑ Ⓒ Ⓓ
   A. and also the teachers
   B. and the teachers was
   C. and the teachers were
   D. but also the teachers were

7. He exercises regularly, _____ he is in good health.

   A. so   Ⓐ Ⓑ Ⓒ Ⓓ
   B. but
   C. yet
   D. for

8. I hope to go to college _____.

   A. and study economic   Ⓐ Ⓑ Ⓒ Ⓓ
   B. or to study economics
   C. and also to study economics
   D. and study economics

9. She wants to take either _____ next semester.

   A. physics nor chemistry   Ⓐ Ⓑ Ⓒ Ⓓ
   B. physics and chemistry
   C. physics or chemistry
   D. physic or chemistry

10. Air _____.

    Ⓐ Ⓑ Ⓒ Ⓓ
    A. both contains oxygen and water
    B. contains both oxygen and water
    C. both oxygen and water contains
    D. both contain oxygen and water

Agreement and Parallel Structure

B **Find the underlined word or phrase, A, B, C, or D, that is incorrect. Mark your answer by darkening the oval with the same letter.**

1. <u>Each</u> <u>of the students</u> in the class <u>have</u>
     A   B   C
   <u>a grammar book</u> and a reading book.
        D

   Ⓐ Ⓑ Ⓒ Ⓓ

2. <u>Having</u> <u>a cold</u> can make you feel tired,
     A   B
   <u>miserable</u>, and <u>weakness</u>.
     C   D

   Ⓐ Ⓑ Ⓒ Ⓓ

3. The number of <u>students</u> <u>who</u> passed the
                 A   B
   test <u>were</u> <u>fewer</u> than expected.
       C   D

   Ⓐ Ⓑ Ⓒ Ⓓ

4. Mathematics <u>are</u> my favorite class, <u>but</u>
             A   B
   I also <u>like</u> <u>physics</u> and chemistry.
         C   D

   Ⓐ Ⓑ Ⓒ Ⓓ

5. <u>The principal of the school</u>, <u>along with</u>
           A   B
   the teachers <u>and</u> custodians, <u>were</u> present
             C   D
   at the meeting.

   Ⓐ Ⓑ Ⓒ Ⓓ

6. <u>The news</u> about the economy <u>are</u> <u>both</u> a
     A   B   C
   surprise <u>and</u> a relief.
         D

   Ⓐ Ⓑ Ⓒ Ⓓ

7. <u>Each of the students</u> agreed <u>that</u>
         A   B
   twenty minutes <u>are</u> <u>not enough</u> for an
                C   D
   essay exam.

   Ⓐ Ⓑ Ⓒ Ⓓ

8. Many people in the world <u>has</u> <u>neither</u>
                        A   B
   food to eat <u>nor</u> clean <u>water</u> to drink.
            C   D

   Ⓐ Ⓑ Ⓒ Ⓓ

9. Our teacher <u>expects us</u> to be <u>on time</u>,
             A   B
   <u>to do</u> all our homework, and <u>sitting</u>
    C   D
   quietly in class.

   Ⓐ Ⓑ Ⓒ Ⓓ

10. <u>Everybody</u> in our class <u>enjoy</u> <u>doing</u>
       A   B   C
    <u>quizzes</u>.
      D

    Ⓐ Ⓑ Ⓒ Ⓓ

UNIT 11

NOUN CLAUSES AND REPORTED SPEECH

11a Noun Clauses Beginning with *That*

I hope **that I have passed the test.**

Main Clause	Noun Clause (with *That*)
I think	**(that) she's a movie star.**
She hopes	**(that) people won't notice.**

1. Noun clauses act as nouns in a sentence. In this unit, most of the noun clauses act as objects. In the first example in the chart, the noun clause *that she is a movie star* is the object of the verb *think*.

2. We use an object noun clause with a main clause. The main clause always comes first. We do not use a comma between the two clauses.

Function

1. We use *that* clauses after certain verbs that express feelings, thoughts, and opinions. Here are some of them.

agree	expect	hope	presume	remember
assume	fear	imagine	pretend	suppose
believe	feel	know	prove	suspect
decide	figure out	learn	read	show
discover	find	notice	realize	teach
doubt	forget	observe	recognize	think
dream	guess	predict	regret	understand

2. We often omit *that* from a noun clause, especially when we speak. The meaning of the sentence does not change.

> Linda: I think **it's raining.**
> OR I think **that it's raining.**
> John: I hope **we don't get wet.**
> OR I hope **that we don't get wet.**

3. When the introductory verb is in the present tense, the verb in the noun clause can be in the present, past, or future, depending on the meaning of the sentence.

> I believe he**'s** here (now).
> I believe he**'ll** be here (in a few minutes).
> I believe he **was** here (a few minutes ago).

4. In conversation, to avoid repeating the *that* clause after verbs such as *think, believe,* and *hope,* we can use *so* or *not* in response to a yes/no question.

> Ken: Is Nancy here today?
> Pat: I **think so.** (I think that Nancy is here today.)
> Ken: Has the rain stopped?
> Pat: I don't **believe so.** (I don't believe that the rain has stopped.)
> Ken: Are we having dinner soon?
> Pat: I**'m afraid not.** (I want us to have dinner soon, but we are not going to.)

	With These Verbs	Question	Answer
Positive Verb + *So*	think		I **think so.**
	believe		I **believe so.**
	be afraid		I'm **afraid so.**
	guess		I **guess so.**
	hope	Has the rain stopped?	I **hope so.**
Negative Verb + *So*	think		I don't **think so.**
	believe		I don't **believe so.**
Positive Verb + *Not*	be afraid		I'm **afraid not.**
	guess		I **guess not.**
	hope		I **hope not.**

5. In formal English, a noun clause can also be the subject of a sentence. In this case we cannot omit the word *that*.

That prices are going up is clear.

It is more common to say the same thing with the word *it* as the subject and with the noun clause at the end.

It is clear **(that) prices are going up.**

1 Practice

Match the two halves of the sentences to make predictions about the future.

What will happen by the year 2050?

___d___ **1.** Population experts predict

_____ **2.** Food scientists expect

_____ **3.** Energy scientists think

_____ **4.** Astronauts will prove

_____ **5.** Robots will figure out

_____ **6.** People will realize

a. that renewable energy will replace fossil fuels.

b. that they are smarter than humans.

c. that it is possible to survive on Mars.

d. that the world's population will be over 9 billion.

e. that everyone needs to speak one language.

f. that most of our food will be genetically modified.

2 What Do You Think?

With a partner, ask and answer the questions. Answer with *think, believe, be afraid, guess,* or *hope* + *so* or *not*.

1. Will the world's population continue to increase?

2. Will hunger in the world disappear by the year 2050?

3. Will people stop using cars?

4. Will scientists figure out a way for humans to live on Mars?

5. Should everyone speak the same language?

3 Your Turn

Write five predictions about the future. Use verbs from the list.

discover   expect   predict   prove   think

Example:
I predict that everyone will learn English on the Internet by the year 2050.

1. _____

2. _____

3. _____

4. _____

5. _____

11b Noun Clauses Beginning with Wh- Words (Indirect Wh- Questions)

Form

I don't know **why he takes his computer on camping trips.**

Main Clause	Noun Clause (Indirect Question)*
She wanted to know	**who I was.**
	where they came from.
	why he called.
I don't know	**when he arrives.**
	what she said.
	how they did it so fast.

Indirect question is the name of this type of noun clause.

1. Noun clauses may also begin with wh- words. Sentences with noun clauses beginning with wh- words are also called indirect questions.

   Direct Question: Why did he call?
   Indirect Question: I don't know why he called.

2. Although wh- clauses begin with a question word, they do not follow question word order. Instead, they use statement word order.

   CORRECT: I know where **she is**.
   INCORRECT: I know where ~~is she~~.

3. We use a question mark at the end of a sentence if the main clause is a direct question and a period at the end of a sentence if the main clause is a statement.

	Main Clause	Noun Clause (Indirect Question)
Main clause is a question	**Can you tell me**	where the elevators are?
Main clause is a statement	**I wonder**	where the elevators are.

1. We usually use an indirect question to express something we do not know or to express uncertainty.

> I don't know **how much it is**.

2. We often use indirect questions to ask politely for information.

> Direct Question: What time does the train leave?
> Indirect Question: Can you tell me what time the train leaves?

4 Practice

Rewrite each question as a main clause + a wh- noun clause. Be sure to use correct punctuation at the end of the sentences.

You are going to a job interview. What questions will you ask?

1. How many people does your company employ?

   Can you tell me *how many people the company employs?*

2. When did the company first get started?

   I'd like to know _____

3. Where is the head office?

   Can you tell me _____

4. What are the job benefits?

   Can you tell me _____

5. How many vacation days do people get?

   I wonder _____

6. What is the salary?

   Can you tell me _____

7. Who will my manager be?

   I'd like to know _____

8. When does the job start?

   Can you tell me _____

9. How many people are you going to interview for this job?

Can you tell me _____

10. When can you tell me the results of this interview?

If you don't mind, I'd like to know _____

5 Practice

Rewrite each direct question as an indirect question (a main clause + a wh- noun clause). Be sure to use correct punctuation at the end of the sentences.

You have a job interview tomorrow, and you are asking a friend to help you prepare. Your friend is telling you about the questions that they will probably ask you.

1. They will probably ask _what your current job title is._
(What is your current job title?)

2. They will want to know _____
(What are your job duties?)

3. They will ask _____
(What qualifications do you have?)

4. They will want to know _____
(Who was your previous employer?)

5. They will ask _____
(How long did you work in your last job?)

6. They will want to know _____
(Why did you leave your last job?)

7. They will ask _____
(What was your salary?)

8. They will want to know _____
(Why do you want the job?)

9. They will ask _____
(How did you find out about the job?)

10. They will want to know _____
(When can you start work?)

Your Turn

Work with a partner. Think of an unusual job. Imagine that you went to a job
interview for this job and write five wh- questions the interviewer asked you.
Tell the class about the questions using a main clause + a wh- noun clause.
Your classmates should guess the job.

Example:
(The unusual job was a lion tamer.)
They asked (me) why I was interested in lions.

11c Noun Clauses Beginning with *If* or *Whether* (Indirect Yes/No Questions)

Form

I wonder **if he understands me.**

Yes/No Question	Main Clause	Noun Clause (Indirect Yes/No Question)
Did he see you?	Do you know	**if/whether he saw you (or not)?**
Are they angry?	I don't know	**if/whether they're angry (or not).**
Is she at home?	I wonder	**if/whether she's at home (or not).**

1. Noun clauses with *if* or *whether* are indirect yes/no questions.

   Direct Question: Are they angry?
   Indirect Question: I don't know if they are angry or not.

2. *If* and *whether* noun clauses must begin with *if* or *whether*. They do not follow
   question word order. Instead, they use statement word order.

   CORRECT: Do you know if this is the director's office?
   INCORRECT: Do you know ~~is this~~ the director's office?

3. We can add the phrase *or not* to the end of an *if/whether* clause if the clause is short.

> I don't know if she's here **or not**.
> I don't know whether she is here **or not**.

We can also put *or not* immediately after *whether,* but not after *if*.

> CORRECT: I don't know whether or not she is here.
> INCORRECT: I don't know if ~~or not~~ she's here.

Function

1. *If* and *whether* at the beginning of a noun clause have the same meaning. We usually use *whether* in more formal situations.

2. We usually use *if/whether* clauses following verbs of mental activity.

> I can't remember **if I turned off my computer**.
> I wonder **whether he has sent me a message**.

3. We use *if/whether* clauses in polite questions.

> Do you know **if Mr. Gallo is in the office today**?
> Can you tell me **whether Flight 213 has arrived or not**?

---

7 Practice

Rewrite each question as a main clause + an *if/whether* noun clause. Be sure to use correct punctuation at the end of the sentences.

You are thinking of having a birthday party at the Paradise Restaurant. Ask your friend about the restaurant.

A: Did we eat lunch there together last year, or didn't we?

B: I can't remember *if we ate lunch there together last year.*
                                        1

A: Did we like the food?

B: I can't remember _____
                                        2

A: Are they open for lunch on Saturday?

B: I don't know _____
                                        3

A: Is there a fixed price lunch menu?

B: We can ask _____
4

A: Are there enough tables for fifty guests?

B: I don't know _____
5

A: Do they have live music?

B: I can't say _____
6

A: Can they order a special birthday cake?

B: I wonder _____
7

A: Do they have a vegetarian meal option?

B: I'm not sure _____
8

A: Do they have high chairs for children?

B: I wonder _____
9

A: Is it a good idea to go there, or isn't it?

B: We need to decide _____
10

8 Your Turn

Work with a partner. Imagine that you are planning to stay at an expensive hotel. Your friend knows the hotel quite well. Ask your friend five questions about the hotel.

Example:
You: I wonder if they have a sports center.
Your partner: Of course. They have a huge sports center with an Olympic-sized pool.

11d Quoted Speech

James Dean said, **"Dream as if you'll live forever. Live as if you'll die today."** He died at the age of 24 when his car crashed.

1. See page 258 for punctuation rules for quoted speech.

2. We use quoted speech to show the exact words someone uses. We use quoted speech in novels, stories, and newspaper articles. In these examples, notice where the "said" phrase is. Notice that it can go before or after its subject.

Story about James Dean:	"Dream as if you'll live forever. Live as if you'll die today," **James Dean said.**
	OR **James Dean said,** "Dream as if you'll live forever. Live as if you'll die today."
Newspaper article:	"I will not vote for this law," **said Senator Smith.**

9 Practice

Read the following fable from Aesop. Use the correct punctuation and capitalization for quoted speech. Note that when the speaker changes, we start a new paragraph.

The Travelers and the Sea

Two travelers were walking along the seashore. They saw something far out on the waves.

"Look," said one. "There is a big ship coming from far away with gold and riches on it."

The object they saw came nearer to the shore.

No said the other that's not a treasure ship. It's a fisherman's boat with the day's catch of good fish

The object came even nearer to the shore. The waves washed it up on the shore.

It's a chest of gold lost from a shipwreck they both said. Both travelers rushed to the beach, but they found nothing but a wet piece of wood.

Moral: Do not let your hopes carry you away from reality.

Practice

Read the story. Use the correct punctuation and capitalization for quoted speech.

The Travelers and the Purse

Two men were traveling together along a road when one of them picked up a purse.

"How lucky I am," he said, "I've found a purse. Judging by its weight it must be full of gold."

Don't say *I* have found a purse said his companion. Instead, say *we* have found a purse and how lucky *we* are. Travelers should share the fortunes and misfortunes of the road

No, no replied the other angrily. *I* found it and *I* am going to keep it

Just then they heard a shout of "Stop! Thief!" and when they looked around, they saw a mob of people with clubs coming down the road.

The man who had found the purse began to panic.

We'll be in trouble if they find the purse on us he said

No, no replied the other you wouldn't say *we* before, so now stick to your *I*.

Say *I* am in trouble

Moral: We cannot expect anyone to share our misfortunes unless we are willing to share our good fortunes also.

Your Turn

Write what your teacher said in class today in quoted speech.

Example:
My teacher said, "I want you to do all the exercises on quoted speech by the next lesson."

◆ 11e Reported Speech: Statements

Form

Benjamin Franklin said **that nothing was certain except death and taxes.**

1. *Say* and *tell* are examples of reporting verbs. If a reporting verb is in the present, there is no change in tense in reported speech. We can omit *that* with no change in meaning.

> Quoted Speech: Mary **says**, "I **am** happy."
> Reported Speech: Mary **says** (that) she **is** happy.

2. If the reporting verb is in the past tense (*said, told*), the verb tense changes when we report it. Here are some common tense changes.

Quoted Speech	Reported Speech
Mary said, "I **do** all the work."	Mary said that she **did** all the work.
Mary said, "I**'m doing** all the work."	Mary said that she **was doing** all the work.
Mary said, "I **did** all the work."	Mary said that she **had done** all the work.
Mary said, "I**'ve done** all the work."	Mary said that she **had done** all the work.
Mary said, "I**'ve been doing** all the work."	Mary said that she **had been doing** all the work.
Mary said, "I**'ll do** all the work."	Mary said that she **would do** all the work.
Mary said, "I **can do** all the work."	Mary said that she **could do** all the work.

3. Pronouns can change in reported speech. The change depends on the meaning. Here are some common examples.

	Quoted	Reported	Quoted Example	Reported Example
Subject Pronouns	I	he, she	Sam said, "**I**'m leaving."	Sam said that **he** was leaving. (Sam was leaving.)
	you (singular)	I	Sam said, "**You**'re leaving."	Sam said that **I** was leaving. (The speaker is leaving.)
		he, she	Sam said, "**You**'re leaving."	Sam said that **he** was leaving. (Sam was talking to a boy or a man.)
	we	they	Sam said, "**We**'re tired."	Sam said that **they** were tired. (*They* includes Sam and other people.)
	you (plural)	we	Sam said, "**You**'re tired."	Sam said that **we** were tired. (*We* includes Sam and other people, but not Sam.)
		they	Sam said, "**You**'re tired."	Sam said that **they** were tired. (*They* includes a group of other people, but not Sam or the speaker.)

	Quoted	Reported	Quoted Example	Reported Example
Object Pronouns	me	him, her	Sam said, "It's for **me**."	Sam said that it was for **him**. (It was for Sam.)
	you (singular)	me	Sam said, "It's for **you**."	Sam said that it was for **me**. (It was for the speaker.)
		him, her	Sam said, "It's for **you**."	Sam said that it was for him/her. (Sam was talking to a man/woman.)
	us	us	Sam said, "It's for **us**."	Sam said that it was for **us**. (*Us* includes the speaker.)
		them	Sam said, "It's for **us**."	Sam said that it was for **them**. (*Us* includes Sam, but not the speaker.)
	you (plural)	us	Sam said, "It's for **you**."	Sam said that it was for **us**. (*Us* includes the speaker and other people, but not Sam.)
		them	Sam said, "It's for **you**."	Sam said that it was for **them**. (*Them* includes other people, but not Sam or the speaker.)
Possessive Forms	my	his, her	Sam said, "**My** son is sleepy."	Sam said that **his** son was sleepy. (The son is the speaker's.)
	your (singular)	my	Sam said, "**Your** son is sleepy."	Sam said that **my** son was sleepy. (The son is the speaker's.)
		his, her	Sam said, "**Your** son is sleepy."	Sam said that **her** son was sleepy. (The son belongs to a woman, not Sam or the speaker.)
	our	their	Sam said, "We have a gift for **our** neighbors."	Sam said that they had a gift for **their** neighbors. (The neighbors are not the speaker's.)
	your (plural)	our	Sam said, "**Your** garden is beautiful."	Sam said that **our** garden was beautiful. (The garden belongs to the speaker and other people.)
		their	Sam said, "**Your** garden is beautiful."	Sam said that **their** garden was beautiful. (The garden belongs to other people, but not Sam or the speaker.)

4. Time expressions can also change in reported speech. Again, it depends on the meaning. Here are come common changes.

Quoted	Reported
now	then
today	that day
tonight	that night
yesterday	the day before
tomorrow	the next day
this week/month/year	that week/month/year
last week/month/year	the week/month/year before
next week/month/year	the week/month/year after
two weeks/months/years ago	two weeks/months/years before

Quoted Speech: She said, "I'm going on vacation **today**."
Reported Speech: She said that she was going on vacation **that day**.

Quoted Speech: Tom explained, "I finished all of the work **yesterday**."
Reported Speech: Tom explained that he had finished all of the work **the day before**.

5. Here are two additional common changes.

Quoted	Reported
here	there
come	go

Quoted Speech: They said, "We'll be **here** when you arrive."
Reported Speech: They said that they would be **there** when we arrived.

Quoted Speech: My mother said, "I hope you can **come** over for dinner."
Reported Speech: My mother said that she hoped I could **go** over for dinner.

| 12 | Practice

It's a very busy time at the office, so the manager asked the staff to work on Saturday morning. Report the answers the staff gave him.

1. Susan said, "I can't work because I am having my car fixed and won't be able to get here."

    Susan said that she couldn't work on Saturday because she was

    having her car fixed and she wouldn't be able to get there.

2. Mary Ann said, "I have made other arrangements, and I can't change them now."

_____

3. Ted explained, "I'll be out of town. I'm taking my children to see their grandparents."

_____

_____

4. Stanley complained, "I'm too tired. I need Saturday and Sunday to relax."

_____

_____

5. Steve insisted, "I'll work on Saturday morning, but only if I get paid double."

_____

_____

6. Kate wondered, "Why do I have to come in if the others aren't?"

_____

_____

7. You said, "_____ "

_____

_____

13 Practice

Your friend is in the hospital, and she can't call her telephone answering service. She has asked you to listen to her phone messages. Write the messages using reported speech.

Message 1:

This is Cindy from the dentist's office. I'm calling to remind you that you have a dental appointment tomorrow at 10:00.

Cindy called from the dentist's office. She was calling to remind you that you have a dental appointment tomorrow at 10:00.

Message 2:

Hi, it's Janet. I just want to say hello. I'll call you later.

_____

_____

Message 3:

My name is Ken Stevens. I've been trying to reach you to talk about the new work schedule. My number is 678-9542. Please call me back.

_____

_____

Message 4:

This is Tony from the Travel Shop. Your tickets will be ready tomorrow. If you'd like us to mail them to you, we can send them by regular mail or express mail. Let me know.

_____

_____

Message 5:

It's Jim. My boss gave me two tickets for the Wild Rockers concert next week.
Do you want to go with me?

_____

_____

Message 6:

It's your mother, dear. I called you at work and you weren't there. I've been calling you at home, but there is no answer. Where are you? I'm worried. Please call me.

_____

_____

Message 7:

It's Mother again. It has been twenty-four hours, and I still haven't heard from you. Something has to be wrong. Please call me.

_____

_____

14 | Your Turn

What interesting things did people say to you yesterday? Use reported speech.

Example:
My friend told me that he saw Ben Affleck in the street yesterday.

11f Reported Speech: Questions

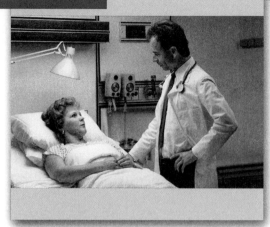

The doctor asked **how I felt.**

1. Like indirect questions, questions in reported speech use statement word order.

   Direct Question: Will it rain this afternoon?
   Indirect Question: I want to know if it will rain this afternoon.
   Reported Question: She asked me if it would rain this afternoon.

   Direct Question: Where is my CD player?
   Indirect Question: She wonders where her CD player is.
   Reported Question: She asked me where her CD player was.

2. Reported questions use a reporting verb such as *ask*. They report someone else's words.

3. Reported questions use the same tense, pronoun, and time expression changes as reported statements (see page 119).

4. After *ask,* we can use an object (*me, Nancy*) to say who asked the question.

   I **asked Nancy** if she was* busy.
   He **asked me** where I had gone.
   He **asked** to leave early.

5. After the verb *tell* we must use an object.

   CORRECT: He told me what he wanted.
   INCORRECT: He told what he wanted.

*In formal English, *was* would be *were.*

15 Practice

Sue lived in Los Angeles for a few years, and now she is back in her home town. She meets an old friend named Jeff. Rewrite Sue's questions as reported questions.

1. Jeff: How are you?

   He asked her how she was.

2. Jeff: When did you get back?

   _____

3. Jeff: Did you like Los Angeles?

   _____

4. Jeff: Why didn't you stay there longer?

   _____

5. Jeff: Are you living in your old neighborhood?

   _____

6. Jeff: Are you still living alone?

   _____

7. Jeff: What are you doing for a living now?

   _____

8. Jeff: Would you like to play tennis with me again, like old times?

   _____

9. Jeff: Do you have the same cell phone number?

   _____

10. Jeff: Can I call you tonight?

   _____

16 Your Turn

Think of four questions to ask your partner about his/her future. Your partner will answer your questions. Then, you will report to the class what you wanted to know and your partner's answers.

Example:

You:	What subject do you want to study in college?
Your partner:	I want to study chemistry.
You:	Where do you want to study?
Your partner:	At the state university.
You:	I asked my partner what subject she wanted to study. She told me that she wanted to study chemistry. I also asked her where she wanted to study, and she answered that she wanted to study at the state university.

11g Reported Commands, Requests, Offers, Advice, Invitations, and Warnings

Form / Function

The police officer warned me **not to do** it again.

VERB + OBJECT + (NOT) + INFINITIVE

	Quoted Speech	Reported Speech			
		Subject	Verb	(Object)	(*Not* +) Infinitive
Commands	"Wait."	They	**told**	**me**	**to wait.**
	"Don't get lost."	She	**told**	**us**	**not to get** lost.
Requests	"Talk quietly, please."	We	**asked**	**them**	**to (please) talk** quietly.
	"Could you not drive so fast?"	I	**asked**	**him**	**not to drive** so fast.
Advice	"You should call her."	He	**advised**	**me**	**to call** her.
	"We shouldn't eat so much."	She	**advised**	**us**	**not to eat** so much.
Invitations	"Would you like to have lunch with us?"	They	**asked**	**me**	**to have** lunch with them.
Warnings	"You'd better not be late."	She	**warned**	**them**	**not to be** late.
	"We'd better be careful."	He	**warned**	**us**	**to be** careful.

VERB + (*NOT*) + INFINITIVE

	Quoted Speech	Reported Speech		
		Subject	Verb	(*Not* +) Infinitive
Threats	"I won't give you the money."	She	**threatened**	**not to give** me the money.
Promises	"I'll take you to the movies tomorrow."	I	**promised**	**to take** her to the movies the next day.
Offers	"Can I help you?"	He	**offered**	**to help** me.

Notice that the verbs *tell, ask, advise,* and *warn* are followed by an object + (*not*) + an infinitive.

Tell, advise, and *warn* must be followed by an object.

> CORRECT: They told us to come early.
> INCORRECT: They told to come early.

We can use *ask* with or without an object.

> WITH OBJECT: George asked Alex to play the guitar. (George wants Alex to play the guitar.)
> WITHOUT OBJECT: George asked to play the guitar. (George asked permission to play the guitar.)

17 Practice

Rewrite the following sentences using the reporting verbs in parentheses.

Your teacher is giving some instructions before a test.

1. Listen carefully. (tell)

   He told us to listen carefully.

2. Don't talk. (tell)

   _____

3. Please put all your books and papers away. (ask)

   _____

4. Please do not try to copy your neighbor's work. (ask)

   _____

5. I will tell the boss if you use the company car for personal business again. (threaten)

   _____

6. Cheating will be severely punished. (warn)

   _____

7. Check the answers carefully before handing in your paper. (advise)

   _____

8. You will get a prize if you finish all the questions. (promise)

_____

9. Would someone like to help me give out the papers? (invite)

_____

10. Would you like me to repeat the instructions? (offer)

_____

---

18 **Your Turn**

Choose a verb from the list. Say or write a sentence that corresponds to one of the verbs in the list, but do not use the verb in your sentence. Ask a partner to guess which verb you chose. Continue with other verbs from the list.

advise	ask	invite	offer
promise	tell	threaten	warn

Example:
I will help you with your homework, if you do the dishes. (corresponds to a promise)

11h The Subjunctive in Noun Clauses

Our teacher demanded that the class **be** quiet.

1. The subjunctive form is the base form of the verb. It has no present, past, or future form. It has no singular or plural. We put _not_ before the base verb to form the negative.

2. We use the subjunctive form in *that* clauses following certain verbs of command, urgency, or request. Here are some verbs that are followed by the subjunctive in noun clauses.

advise	desire	request
ask	insist	require
command	propose	suggest
demand	recommend	urge

Our teacher **insists** that we **be** on time.
The officer **asked** that he **show** his passport.
They **recommended** that he **not try** to fix the computer himself.

3. We can also use *should* after the verbs *suggest* and *recommend*.

I **suggested** that she **should take** the test soon.

4. We also use the subjunctive form in *that* clauses following adjectives of urgency. These statements are similar to commands, but they are impersonal and therefore softer.

It's **vital** that you **make** a decision right now.   (impersonal and softer)
Make a decision right now!   (strong)
I insist that you make a decision right now.   (strong)

Here are some adjectives of urgency.

advisable	critical	essential	important	urgent
best	desirable	imperative	necessary	vital

19 Practice

Rewrite the following sentences using the subjunctive.

A 17-year-old boy was arrested for stealing CDs from a music store. He was sent to a youth correctional facility for two months. What were the opinions of different people involved in the case?

1. The judge: Go to jail for two months.

   The judge recommended *that he go to jail for two months.*

2. The parents: He must get another trial.

The parents demanded _____

3. The lawyer: Why doesn't he do community service?

The lawyer suggested _____

4. The police officer: He must repay the money to the store owner.

The police officer insisted _____

5. The store owner: Could he please return the CDs?

The store owner requested _____

6. What is your opinion?

I recommend _____

20 Practice

Write one solution for each of the problems. Use the subjunctive and verbs from the list.

create	improve	reduce	stop
develop	protect	restrict	try

1. Many wildlife species are endangered.

It is urgent _____

2. We are running out of fossil fuel.

It is imperative _____

3. Our cities are overcrowded.

It is desirable _____

4. There are too many cars.

It is essential _____

5. Our climate is heating up too rapidly.

It is critical _____

6. We produce too much plastic waste.

It is advisable _____

7. Too many people are dying from hunger.

It is vital _____

8. There are too many wars.

It is critical _____

21 **Your Turn**

In groups, choose one of the following cases. Imagine the opinions of different people involved in the case. Say and write sentences about the case using *recommend, insist, suggest,* **and** *demand.*

Example:
The train conductor insisted that the boy get off at the next station.

1. A 15-year-old boy was traveling on a train alone. He didn't have a ticket. (boy, train conductor, other passengers)

2. A friend of yours spent over three thousand dollars on a credit card to buy luxury clothes and jewelry. (friends, you)

3. A man pretended that his car had been stolen so that he could claim insurance. Actually, the car had broken down and he couldn't afford to repair it. (man, insurance company, representative, man's wife)

_____

_____

_____

_____

_____

_____

_____

_____

_____

REVIEW

1 **Review (11a–11c, 11e–11g)**

Rewrite the quotes as reported speech.

1. Cindy said, "Matthew, get out of bed, or you'll be late for your interview."

   Cindy told <u>Matthew to get out of bed or he'd be late for</u>

   <u>his interview.</u>

2. Matthew said, "Why didn't you get me up earlier?"

   Matthew wanted to know _____

3. Cindy said, "I went to the gym."

   Cindy said that _____

4. Matthew said, "Did I set my alarm clock or not?"

   Mathew couldn't remember _____

5. Cindy suggested, "Matthew, you'd better hurry if you want to get that job."

   Cindy suggested that _____

6. The interviewer had said, "Be here on time."

   The interviewer had insisted _____

7. Cindy said, "Why did you sleep so late?"

   Cindy said she didn't understand _____

8. Matthew explained, "I was preparing for the interview until 2:00 A.M."

   Matthew explained that _____

9. Cindy asked, "How do you expect to get there, Matthew?"

   Cindy asked _____

10. Matthew asked, "Can you drive me there?"

    Matthew wondered if _____

11. Cindy asked, "How far is it to the office?"

    Cindy wanted to know _____

12. Matthew said, "It's about 20 miles."

    Matthew explained that _____

2 Review (IIa–IIc, IIe–IIg)

Rewrite the quotes as reported speech.

1. Michael asked, "Are we going to the museum today, Susan?"

   Michael asked Susan _if they were going to the museum._

2. Susan asked, "Could you get my umbrella?"

   Susan asked _____

3. Michael asked, "Is it raining now?"

   Michael wanted to know _____

4. Michael asked, "Is the museum open on Mondays?"

   Michael wanted to know _____

5. Susan said, "I'm really excited about seeing the new abstract art exhibit."

   Susan said _____

6. Michael said, "My car isn't running."

   Michael said _____

7. Susan said, "Don't worry because my mother can take us."

   Susan told _____

8. Michael suggested, "Let's go by bus."

   Michael suggested _____

9. Susan asked, "What time does the next bus come?"

   Susan wanted to know _____

10. Michael said, "It'll be here in five minutes."

    Michael told Susan _____

11. Michael said, "Did I give you the discount tickets?"

    Michael couldn't remember _____

12. Susan said, "Don't look for them now."

    Susan recommended _____

13. Susan warned, "We'll miss the bus."

    Susan warned Michael that _____

Read the following fable from West Africa. Find and correct the errors in noun clauses and quoted and reported speech.

Ananse lived with his family. One year there was no rain, so the crops did not grow.
Ananse ~~that~~ knew ^*that* there would not be enough food to feed everyone. One day his wife

asked Will it rain at all this summer?

I don't believe so he replied. You know, I prefer to die than to see my children starve.

Therefore, I will allow myself to die so that there will be enough food for the family.

Ananse then told to his wife that he wants the family to bury me on the farm and to put

into my coffin all the things I will need for my journey into the next world. He said, "It's

critical that you left my grave open. I want my soul to be free to wander. And I insist that

no one visits the farm for three months after my death.

The next morning, Ananse's family found him dead. But Ananse was only pretending.

At night he would lift the lid of his coffin and take food from the farm. One day his son,

Ntikuma, realized that there wasn't much food in the house and that he must visit the farm

to get some. He said he needed to go today to get what little food the farm had to feed

the family. Where is all the corn and millet? he said to himself when he got to the farm.

His mother told him the food was disappearing at night. It's a thief exclaimed Ntikuma.

I want to know who is he.

Ntikuma carved a statue from wood and covered it with tar*. Then he placed the

figure in the field. That evening, Ananse came out of his coffin and saw the figure. Good

evening he said. I don't know you. Please tell me who are you? The figure did not reply.

Ananse got angry, so he slapped the figure. His hand stuck fast. Ananse shouted If I don't

let go of my right hand, he'll hit you with his left! He hit the figure with his left hand. He

hit the statue with his right leg, then the left. Ananse struggled as the figure fell. He was

stuck was very clear.

*tar: a dark, thick, sticky petroleum-based material used, for example, to build roads and roofs

The next day Ntikuma and others went to the field. I wonder Ananse caught the thief someone asked. Then they found Ananse. He was so ashamed he didn't know what to do, so he turned into a spider and climbed up a tree where he could not be seen.

This story is a West African fable meant to teach a lesson about selfishness.

4 Review (11c–11e, 11h)

Find and correct the errors in noun clauses and quoted and reported speech.

"I want more excitement," said one traveler.

I want different things to do said another.

When asked, many travelers have insisted that we don't want to do just one thing while we're on vacation. In response, many tour operators now offer combination packages, or "combos." David Rose of High Roads Traveled says We now offer combo packages that mix several activities in one outing. Mr. Rose recommends that a traveler takes a combo if he or she likes fun and adventure. People love these trips is very clear, he adds.

Combo packages mix hiking, cycling, biking, climbing, rafting, horseback riding, or other activities. Ron Clair of Ways Traveled says, "Combos are his most popular trips.

"Sunbathing at the beach all week is a thing of the past, says Margaret Erikson, author of *Your Adventure.* Can I tell you why are combos so popular? she asks. She continues today travelers demand tour operators that will give them a variety of adventures. Will this trend continue? I believe so. Sometimes I wonder the old car trip will eventually fade away.

Some people wonder if or not they must be a superior athlete to take a combo adventure. Top athletes do things on their own says Mary Miller of High Mountain Bike Tours. She adds that my company is oriented toward vacations for the average person. She does say that I talk to a client first and advises he or she prepare. She says, "It's important that you are doing some cycling or hiking before you go on any adventure vacation. But I urge that every client remembers that our tours are designed to be enjoyed at your own pace and in your own style.

Do you know where are you going on your next vacation? If you're into major thrills, a combo adventure just may be what are you looking for.

WRITING: Write a Fable or a Legend

All cultures have stories. A fable is a story that teaches a lesson, which is called a "moral." The moral is usually stated at the end of the fable. In many fables, animals speak and act as humans do. A legend is a story, usually about famous people or events, that is handed down from generation to generation. It may be based in historical reality.

Step 1. Think of a legend or fable that you know. Tell it to your partner. Discuss its meaning to the culture it comes from.

Step 2. Write the events of your story in order.

Step 3. Write the story. Include quoted and reported speech from the characters. Write a title for your story. Here is an example of a fable.

> ### The Fox and the Crow
>
> One day a fox was walking through the forest when he noticed a crow up in a tree. The crow had a piece of cheese in its beak, and the fox was hungry. "That cheese looks delicious," the fox said to himself. He wondered how he could get the cheese. He thought, and then he said, "Good morning, beautiful bird. You are indeed beautiful, and I am sure that you have a beautiful voice. Let me hear you sing." The crow ruffled his feathers and looked proud. Then he opened his beak to sing. Immediately the cheese fell out. The fox snatched it up and ran away.
>
> *Moral: Never trust someone who flatters you.*

Step 4. Evaluate your fable or legend.

Checklist

_____ Did you tell the events in the order in which they occurred?

_____ Did you use quoted and reported speech?

_____ Did you write a title for the story?

_____ If you wrote a fable, did you write a moral at the end?

Step 5. Work with a partner or a teacher to edit your fable or legend. Check spelling, vocabulary, and grammar.

Step 6. Write your final copy.

A Choose the best answer, A, B, C, or D, to complete the sentence. Mark your answer by darkening the oval with the same letter.

1. I wondered where _____.

   A. he came from   Ⓐ Ⓑ Ⓒ Ⓓ
   B. did he come from
   C. came he from
   D. he did come from

2. My mother said, "Don't come in with your dirty shoes."
   My mother warned me _____ in with my dirty shoes.

   A. to come   Ⓐ Ⓑ Ⓒ Ⓓ
   B. not come
   C. not came
   D. not to come

3. I don't know _____ the right place.

   A. is this   Ⓐ Ⓑ Ⓒ Ⓓ
   B. if is this
   C. if this is
   D. this is

4. Ed: Is Jim in his office?
   Kathy: _____.

   A. I think Jim is   Ⓐ Ⓑ Ⓒ Ⓓ
   B. I think
   C. I think so
   D. Yes, Jim is

5. "I'll see you soon," she said. But we didn't see each other for a long time.
   She said _____.

   A. she will see me soon Ⓐ Ⓑ Ⓒ Ⓓ
   B. she would see me soon
   C. I would see her soon
   D. she see me soon

6. "Don't drive too fast."

   He told _____ drive fast.
   A. not to   Ⓐ Ⓑ Ⓒ Ⓓ
   B. to
   C. us not to
   D. to us not to

7. He asked, "Where do you want to go?"
   He asked where _____.

   A. did I want to go   Ⓐ Ⓑ Ⓒ Ⓓ
   B. I want to go
   C. I wanted to go
   D. do I want to go

8. It is urgent that she _____ a decision right now.

   A. makes   Ⓐ Ⓑ Ⓒ Ⓓ
   B. is able to make
   C. make
   D. to make

9. Can you tell me what time _____?

   A. the train arrives   Ⓐ Ⓑ Ⓒ Ⓓ
   B. does the train arrive
   C. the train does it arrive
   D. arrives the train

10. "Have you finished your exams?" he asked. "Yes," I answered.
    He asked _____ my exams.

        Ⓐ Ⓑ Ⓒ Ⓓ
    A. whether I have finished
    B. whether did I finish
    C. if I had finished
    D. if I have finished

B Find the underlined word or phrase, A, B, C, or D, that is incorrect. Mark your answer by darkening the oval with the same letter.

1. The teacher <u>warned</u> <u>us</u> <u>that</u> <u>not to</u> cheat
           A   B   C   D

   during the test.

   Ⓐ Ⓑ Ⓒ Ⓓ

2. The interviewer <u>asked</u> <u>to me</u> when
                A   B

   <u>I wanted</u> to start <u>working</u>.
     C   D

   Ⓐ Ⓑ Ⓒ Ⓓ

3. <u>Can you tell me</u> where <u>can I</u> get
       A   B

   information about trains and <u>where</u>
                            C

   <u>I can</u> buy tickets?
    D

   Ⓐ Ⓑ Ⓒ Ⓓ

4. Paul asked if <u>did</u> they <u>told</u> <u>me</u> when they
              A   B   C

   <u>were leaving</u>.
      D

   Ⓐ Ⓑ Ⓒ Ⓓ

5. <u>Do you know</u> <u>if or not</u> we <u>need</u> <u>to get</u> a
     A   B   C   D

   visa to enter the country?

   Ⓐ Ⓑ Ⓒ Ⓓ

6. Ted <u>said that</u> he <u>hadn't</u> <u>fill out</u> the
        A   B   C

   application form <u>yet</u>.
                 D

   Ⓐ Ⓑ Ⓒ Ⓓ

7. <u>It is</u> <u>imperative that</u> <u>I fail not</u> any of
    A   B   C

   my courses this year <u>if</u> I want to apply
                      D

   to a university.

   Ⓐ Ⓑ Ⓒ Ⓓ

8. Tony called from Boston <u>yesterday</u> and
                      A

   <u>told me</u> that <u>it was</u> extremely cold <u>here</u>.
     B   C   D

   Ⓐ Ⓑ Ⓒ Ⓓ

9. I <u>don't know</u> what <u>did happen</u> to <u>him</u>
      A   B   C

   after I <u>left</u> school.
         D

   Ⓐ Ⓑ Ⓒ Ⓓ

10. He <u>invited</u> <u>us</u> to <u>going</u> to the theater
        A   B   C

    <u>next Sunday</u>.
     D

    Ⓐ Ⓑ Ⓒ Ⓓ

UNIT 12

ADJECTIVE CLAUSES

12a Adjective Clauses with Subject Relative Pronouns

Form / Function

A police officer is a person **who doesn't usually smile on the job.**

1. An adjective clause, like an adjective, describes or gives more information about a noun.

   We have **noisy** neighbors.   (The adjective *noisy* describes the noun *neighbors*.)

   I have neighbors **that are very noisy.**   (The adjective clause *that are very noisy* describes the noun *neighbors*.)

2. We introduce an adjective clause with the relative pronouns *who, whom, that,* or *which*. The relative pronoun refers to a noun in the main clause.

   I have a friend **who** lives in Mexico City.

3. When the relative pronoun comes before the verb in the adjective clause, the relative pronoun is the subject of the clause. It is a subject relative pronoun.

MAIN CLAUSE	ADJECTIVE CLAUSE	
	Subject Relative Pronoun	
I have a friend	**who**	lives in Mexico City.
I have neighbors	**that**	are very noisy.
I live in a building	**that/which**	has very thin walls.

4. We use *who* or *that* to refer to people.

5. We use *which* or *that* to refer to things. In careful writing, some people prefer *that,* not *which,* to refer to things.

See pages 151-152 for information on when we must use *who* or *which,* not *that*.

6. A subject relative pronoun always has the same form. It does not change for singular, plural, feminine, or masculine words.

> That's the **man who** works in my office.
> That's the **woman who** works in my office.
> Those are the **people who** work in my office.

7. The verb in an adjective clause is singular if the subject relative pronoun refers to a singular noun. The verb is plural if it refers to a plural noun.

> Ken is a man **who works** in my office. (*Man* is third person singular, so the verb is also third person singular.)
>
> Tony and Fred are men **who work** in another department. (The noun *men* is plural, so the verb is plural.)

---

1 Practice

Read the paragraphs about inventors and their inventions. Then answer the questions using adjective clauses with subject relative pronouns.

1. Mary Anderson invented the windshield wiper in 1903. She wanted to make streetcars safer in the rain. Her invention allowed the driver to control the wipers from inside the streetcar.

   a. Who was Mary Anderson?

   She was the person _who invented the windshield wiper._

   _____

   b. What was the purpose of her invention?

   She wanted to invent something _____

   _____

2. Contact lenses were first made in 1887 by the German doctor Adolf Fick. His first lenses were for animals and were made from heavy brown glass. In 1889, August Muller made lenses to help people see things at a distance.

a. Who was Adolf Fick?

He was a German doctor _____

_____

b. What kind of lenses did August Muller make for people?

August Muller made lenses _____

_____

3. Levi Strauss and Jacob Davis were tailors. Many people went to California to look for gold in the 1890s. Strauss and Davis sold tents to them. Soon they developed the idea of making workpants from the tent material, and blue jeans were invented. The idea is still popular today.

a. Who were Strauss and Davis?

Strauss and Davis were tailors _____

_____

b. What kind of people bought the tents?

People _____

_____ bought the tents.

c. What kind of pants did they sell?

They sold pants _____

_____

12b Adjective Clauses with Object Relative Pronouns

These are the oranges **that I picked myself.**

1. When the relative pronouns *who (whom), that,* or *which* come before a noun or pronoun, the relative pronoun takes the place of the object. It is an object relative pronoun.

2. When the relative pronoun comes before a noun or a pronoun, the relative pronoun is the object of the adjective clause.

MAIN CLAUSE	ADJECTIVE CLAUSE
Claudia is the woman	**that/who/whom** we met yesterday.
Where is the book	**that** Tom put on the table?

3. We use *that, who,* or *whom* to refer to people. We rarely use *whom* except in formal English.

4. We use *that* or *which* for things.

   See pages 151-152 for information on when we must use *who* or *which,* not *that.*

5. The relative pronoun can be the object of a preposition. In conversational English, we usually put the preposition at the end of a clause and omit the relative pronoun. However, in formal English, we put the preposition at the beginning of the clause. When this is the case, we use *whom* and *which.* We do not use *who* or *that.*

	Main Clause	Adjective Clause
Informal	Where's the person	**who/that** I should speak **to?**
	That's the company	**that/which** we signed the agreement **with.**
Formal	Where is the person	**to whom** I should speak?
	That is the company	**with which** we signed the agreement.

6. We often omit object relative pronouns, especially when we speak.

On the street today, I ran into a man (who/whom) I knew a long time ago.
There's the set of keys (that) I lost yesterday!
Where's the person (that) I should speak to?

But we do not omit subject relative pronouns.

CORRECT: I have a friend **who** lives in Mexico City.
INCORRECT: I have a friend lives in Mexico City.

3 Practice

A. Match the words with the correct definitions.

__h__	**1.** We use this machine to keep food cold.	**a.** bank
_____	**2.** We eat this sauce with burgers and French fries.	**b.** dictionary
_____	**3.** We speak on this machine over long distances.	**c.** doctor
_____	**4.** We ask this person for help when we see a fire.	**d.** firefighter
_____	**5.** We go to this place when we need to borrow a book.	**e.** ketchup
_____	**6.** We use this to see objects far away.	**f.** library
_____	**7.** We look in this book when we need to know the meaning of a word.	**g.** lightbulb
_____	**8.** We use this to see in the dark.	**h.** refrigerator
_____	**9.** We ask this person for help when we are sick.	**i.** telephone
_____	**10.** We go to this place when we need to borrow money.	**j.** telescope

B. Write a sentence using an adjective clause with an object relative pronoun for each item in part A.

1. _A refrigerator is a machine that we use to keep food cold._

2. _____

3. _____

4. _____

5. _____

6. _____

7. _____

8. _____

9. _____

10. _____

4 | Your Turn

Work with a partner. Take turns asking and answering questions with *what* or *who* and the following prompts. Use adjective clauses with object relative pronouns.

Example:
a book you always like to look at

You: What is a book that you always like to look at?
Your partner: *A China Journey* is a book that I always like to look at. It has
                beautiful artwork.

1. something you can't live without
2. a food you always think about
3. a show on TV you always like to watch
4. a person you look up to

5 | Your Turn

Make a list of the three most important inventions of the past 100 years. Then say or write sentences with adjective clauses to describe them. Ask a partner to guess what they are.

Example:
You: It's a machine that you use for storing and working with information.
Your partner: It's a computer.

12c Adjective Clauses with *Whose*

Flamingoes are birds **whose feathers are pink** because of the food they eat.

1. We use the relative pronoun *whose* to show possession. We always use a noun after *whose*. We cannot omit *whose*.

    The English teacher **whose** course I'm taking is walking in front of us.

2. The noun after *whose* is the thing that the person or thing in the main clause possesses.

    That's the student **whose application** we just read.

3. Adjective clauses with *whose* usually show possession for people or animals, but sometimes they refer to things.

    I want to go to the university **whose engineering department** is the best.

4. Do not confuse *whose* with *who's*.

	Meaning	Example
Who's	who is	I know a man **who's** from Egypt.
Whose	shows possession	I know a man **whose** family is in Egypt.

Practice

Combine the sentences using *whose* in an adjective clause.

1. Martin Luther King, Jr., was a civil rights leader. His most famous speech contains the words "I have a dream."

   Martin Luther King, Jr., was a
   civil rights leader whose most
   famous speech contains the words
   "I have a dream."

2. Abraham Lincoln was a president of the United States. His most famous achievement was freeing African-Americans from slavery.

   _____

   _____

3. Benjamin Franklin was an American statesman and inventor. His most famous invention was the lightning rod.

   _____

   _____

4. Wilbur and Orville Wright were brothers. Their aircraft was the first wooden, piloted, heavier-than-air, self-propelled machine to fly.

   _____

   _____

5. Dorothea Lange was a photographer. Her photos made people realize the poverty of workers during the Great Depression.

   _____

   _____

6. Alice Walker is an African-American writer. Her novel *The Color Purple* received the Pulitzer Prize in 1983.

   _____

   _____

7. Elizabeth Cady Stanton was a leader of the American women's rights movement. Her lifetime of work helped women gain the right to vote in the United States.

_____

_____

8. Neil Armstrong was an astronaut. His most famous achievement was walking on the moon.

_____

_____

7	Your Turn

Say or write sentences about other famous people that you know about.

12d *When, Where, Why,* and *That* as Relative Pronouns

Form / Function

Holland is a place **where people wear clogs.**

1. We can use *when* and *where* to introduce an adjective clause.

Relative Pronoun	Function	Example
Where	refers to a place	That's the building **where** he works.
When	refers to a time	I remember the day **when** I met you.

Notice that the relative pronouns *where* and *when* can be replaced with *that* or *which* + a preposition.

> That's the building **where** he works. =
> That's the building **(that)** he works **in**. (OR **in which he works**)

> I remember the day **when** I met you. =
> I remember the day **(that)** I met you **on**. (OR **on which I met you**)

2. When we use *where* or *when*, we do not use a preposition in the adjective clause.

> CORRECT: That's the building where he works. (no preposition)
> INCORRECT: That's the building where he works ~~in~~.

3. After the word *reason,* we can use *why* or *that* in an adjective clause.

> Is there a reason **why/that** you want to go to that university?

4. We can omit *when, why,* and *that* without changing the meaning.

> I remember the day I first met you.
> Is there a reason you want to go to that university?

We can also omit *where* if we use a preposition.

> That's the building he works in.

---

8 | Practice

Complete the sentences with the correct relative pronouns: *that, who, where,* *when,* **or** *why.*

A.

In 1666, there was a terrible plague in London. Isaac Newton went to stay in the country ___where___ his mother had a farm. While he was sitting under an apple tree
1

one day, an apple fell on his head. Suddenly, Newton realized the reason _____
2

objects on the earth fall downwards. It is because they are pulled towards the earth's

center by the force of gravity. Newton proposed that gravity was a universal force

_____ holds planets in their orbits. His universal law led to a principle
3

_____ we now take for granted; the same physical laws are true anywhere in
4

the universe. The day _____ an apple fell on Newton's head changed our view
5

of the world and the universe.

B.

Louis Braille was the man _____ invented books for the blind. Louis became
                              1

blind at the age of four. It was a time _____ there were very few schools for the
                                         2

blind. Blind people were not sent to school, but learned skills like weaving and woodwork

so they could earn a living. Louis was sent to a school in Paris _____ there were
                                                                    3

very few books. The books were written with raised letters _____ made them heavy
                                                             4

and difficult to read. Louis invented a code of raised dots _____ he arranged to
                                                               5

represent each letter of the alphabet. The first Braille book was published in 1827.

C.

Alexander Graham Bell is best known for the invention of the telephone. He first

developed the "harmonic telegraph," a device _____ could send a number of
                                                1

telegraph messages at the same time over a single telegraph wire. In 1875, Bell and his

assistant Watson developed this into a machine _____ could transmit the sound
                                                  2

of the human voice. The day _____ Bell first spoke to his assistant in the next
                              3

room changed history forever. Soon after, Bell and Watson went to Philadelphia

_____ they exhibited their invention at the Centennial Exposition, an exhibition
   4

to celebrate America's 100th birthday. Everyone _____ saw the new invention
                                                   5

was amazed at the idea of instant two-way communication.

9 | Your Turn

Use the prompts to describe your feelings. Discuss your answers with a partner.

Example:
A place where I feel peaceful is in my kitchen. It's especially nice at times when I am
cooking dinner for my family.

a place where you feel peaceful
a reason why you feel anxious
a time when you feel happiest

12e Defining and Nondefining Adjective Clauses

My grandmother, **who is seventy**, has just started to drive.

1. There are two kinds of adjective clauses: defining clauses and nondefining clauses.* All of the types of adjective clauses in sections 12a to 12d in this unit have been defining adjective clauses.

2. We use a defining adjective clause to identify nouns. They tell us which person, thing, etc. the speaker means.

   I know the woman **who works at the registration office**.
   (The clause *who works at the registration office* tells us which woman.)

3. We use a nondefining adjective clause to add extra information about the noun it refers to. We can omit this information because it is not necessary to identify the noun. We begin a nondefining clause with the relative pronouns *who(m)*, *which*, or *whose*. The relative clause follows the noun in the main clause that it refers to.

   My grandmother, **who is seventy**, has just passed her driving test.

   The adjective clause *who is seventy* adds extra information about my grandmother. We know which grandmother the speaker means without this information.

4. We use commas before and after a nondefining clause. If a nondefining clause ends a sentence, we do not use a comma after it. We use a period.

   My apartment, **which is in the center of town,** is very small.
   Jane Kendall, **who is one of my best friends,** has decided to live in New York.
   I'm very excited about my vacation, **which begins tomorrow.**

   In speech, we pause before and after a nondefining clause.

   My apartment [pause], **which is in the center of town,** [pause] is very small.

   *These clauses are also called restrictive and nonrestrictive clauses.

5. We use *who, whom, which,* and *whose* as relative pronouns in nondefining clauses. We do not use the relative pronoun *that* in a nondefining clause. We also do not omit relative pronouns in a nondefining clause.

> CORRECT: He gave me the documents, which I put in my briefcase.
> INCORRECT: He gave me the documents, ~~that~~ I put in my briefcase.
> INCORRECT: He gave me the documents, I put in my briefcase.

6. As with defining adjective clauses, we use some forms of nondefining adjective clauses only in formal English.

> **Whom as Object**
> Formal: The college president, **whom** I met last night, will attend our meeting.
> Informal: The college president, **who** I met last night, will attend our meeting.

> **Preposition +** *Which* **or** *Whom*
> Formal: My senator, **from whom** I expect support, has agreed to meet with me.
> Informal: My senator, **who** I expect support from, has agreed to meet with me.

> Formal: This meeting, **for which** I will travel to Washington, will be next week.
> Informal: This meeting, **which** I will travel to Washington for, will be next week.

7. We sometimes use expressions of quantity with *of* in an adjective clause. Examples are *some of, many of, much of, none of, all of, both of, each of, several of, a number of, a little of,* and *a few of.* These are more common in written English than in speech. Note the structure and the use of commas.

> A number of my friends, **some of whom you know,** will be coming tomorrow.
> She gave me a lot of advice, **most of which was not very useful.**

---

10 Practice

Underline the adjective clauses in this reading about fables. Mark defining adjective clauses as *D* and nondefining as *ND*. Add commas as necessary.

                      D
Fables are stories <u>that have animals in them</u>, but the animals behave as people do.

                        ND
The truth is that fables, <u>which seem to be about animals</u>, are really about people.

The animal characters do all the things that people do that can get us into trouble. At the

end of the fable, there is a moral which is the lesson people should learn.

We have all heard of Aesop whose fables are world famous. However, we are not sure if he was the person who wrote them. They say that Aesop who lived a long time ago in Greece was an African slave. Aesop's stories of which he wrote about 350 are short and entertaining. These fables which give us lessons about life have been popular through the ages.

II Practice

A worker is talking about a coworker. Complete the sentences with the words in parentheses and *of which* or *of whom*.

A: Let's go to lunch with Barbara.

B: Not with Barbara. I don't like her.

A: Why not?

B: Well, she always tries to give advice, (most) _____*most of which*_____ is

                                                                 1

   completely useless.

A: That's not so bad.

B: And she talks about all the designer clothes she has, (none) _____

                                                                                2

   we ever see on her. She tells everyone about how much money she spends on things,

   (all) _____ can't be true because we all know how much she makes.

              3

A: I see.

B: She talks about her two "beautiful" children, (both) _____ look

                                                                    4

   like her, and she is definitely not a beauty.

A: Uh-huh.

B: She always talks about choosing a medical school for her son and daughter,

   (neither) _____ are doing very well in high school.

                      5

   She also talks about her wonderful husband and how good he is to her,

   (a little) _____ must be true, because he has put up

                      6

   with her for so many years!

A: Uh-huh. Oh! Hi, Barbara. Would you like to go to lunch . . . with me?

Write a short paragraph of four or five sentences about the teacher, the students, and the lessons in your class. Use defining and nondefining relative clauses.

Example:

My teacher, whose name is Ms. Adams, is a wonderful person. The students in my class, most of whom are my age, find English difficult. The biggest problem that most of us have in English grammar is articles.

12f Using *Which* to Refer to an Entire Clause

Form / Function

She's finished her classes, **which makes her happy.**

1. We can use a nondefining clause with *which* to refer to a whole clause. Look at these sentences.

> Example A: We had to wait for over an hour. **It** made us feel hungry and irritable.
>
> Example B: We had to wait for over an hour, **which** made us feel hungry and irritable.

> Example C: He gave me the money. **This** was very kind of him.
>
> Example D: He gave me the money, **which** was very kind of him.

In examples A and C, the pronouns *it* and *this* refer to the entire sentence that comes before. We can use *which* in the same way, and it can refer to the whole main clause, as in examples B and D.

2. We usually use this form in spoken English and not often in formal writing.

13 | Practice

Combine each sentence in A with the correct follow-up sentence in B.

A.

_c_	**1.**	The teacher encouraged me.
_____	**2.**	The teacher corrected my paper in red ink.
_____	**3.**	She let us use the Internet to do our research.
_____	**4.**	We didn't have tests every week in this class.
_____	**5.**	We wrote about the news of the day.
_____	**6.**	We worked with other students in class.
_____	**7.**	The teacher always paid a lot of attention to us.
_____	**8.**	We lost points when we handed in homework late.

a. That was easier than finding books from the library.

b. This made us feel less pressure.

c. This motivated me to work harder.

d. That made us feel like she cared about us.

e. That helped me make new friends.

f. It made me read newspapers and listen to the news.

g. It meant I had to do my homework on time.

h. That helped me find my mistakes.

B.

Now combine the pairs of ideas into one sentence with *which*. Take turns reading the sentences with a partner. Remember to pause before *which*.

1. *The teacher encouraged me, which motivated me to work harder.*

2. _____

3. _____

4. _____

5. _____

6. _____

7. _____

8. _____

14 Your Turn

Write a sentence that would naturally go with each of the following sentences. Then combine the two using *which*.

1. _I heard the news about the principal of the school._ This was a shock to me.

I heard the news about the principal of the school, which was a shock to me.

2. _____ This was a nice surprise.

_____

3. _____ This made it more difficult.

_____

4. _____ This was very kind of her.

_____

5. _____ This irritated me.

_____

6. _____ This disappointed me.

_____

12g Reduced Adjective Clauses

The man **sitting on his car** has a problem.

1. We can reduce an adjective clause to an adjective phrase. An adjective phrase modifies a noun. An adjective phrase does not have a subject and a verb. Instead, it has a present participle (base verb + -*ing*) for the active voice or a past participle for the passive voice. Remember that regular past participles end in –*ed,* but many past participles are irregular. See page 228 for a list of them.

   Adjective Clause: The girl **who is waiting at the bus stop** is my sister.
   Adjective Phrase: The girl **waiting at the bus stop** is my sister.

   Adjective Clause: The information **that was found on that Website** was incorrect.
   Adjective Phrase: The information **found on that Website** was incorrect.

2. We can only reduce adjective clauses that have a subject relative pronoun.

   Adjective Clause: The man **who is sitting in the corner** is well known.
   Adjective Phrase: The man **sitting in the corner** is well known.

   Adjective Clause: The man **who I sat next to** was well known.
   Adjective Phrase: (Not possible. *Who* is not a subject pronoun in this example.)

3. There are two ways to reduce an adjective clause.

   a. If the adjective clause has a form of *be,* we omit the subject relative pronoun and the form of *be.*

      Clause: Do you know the woman **who is standing by the window**?
      Phrase: Do you know the woman **standing by the window**?

      Clause: The words **that are underlined in red** have errors.
      Phrase: The words **underlined in red** have errors.

b. If there is no form of *be* in the adjective clause, we can omit the subject pronoun and change the verb to the present participle (*-ing* form).

Clause: Anyone **who wants to send a message** can use these computers to do so.
Phrase: Anyone **wanting to send a message** can use these computers to do so.

Clause: The Inuit have about 70 words **that describe different kinds of snow.**
Phrase: The Inuit have about 70 words **describing different kinds of snow.**

4. If the adjective clause is defining, then the adjective phrase is also defining, and we don't put commas around it. But if the adjective clause is nondefining, the adjective phrase is also nondefining, and we must use commas.

Defining Clause: Scientists **who were working before 1898** didn't know about the element radium.
Defining Phrase: Scientists **working before 1898** didn't know about the element radium.

Nondefining Clause: Marie Curie, **who worked at the Sorbonne in Paris,** discovered the element radium in 1898.
Nondefining Phrase: Marie Curie, **working at the Sorbonne in Paris,** discovered the element radium in 1898.

5. If an adjective phrase follows a noun and starts with a noun, we call it an *appositive*. Use commas around an appositive if it is nondefining. Do not use commas if it is defining.

Adjective Clause: Marie Curie, **who was a winner of the Nobel Prize,** discovered radium.
                  Noun   Noun
Appositive: Marie Curie, **a winner of the Nobel Prize,** discovered radium.

15 Practice

Read about the writer Hans Christian Andersen and underline the adjective clauses. Then rewrite the clauses in reduced form using participles or appositives.

famous for his fairy tales
Hans Christian Andersen was a writer who is famous for his fairy tales. He wrote stories

that are well known all over the world like *The Ugly Duckling, The Princess and the Pea,* and

The Little Mermaid. Andersen, who was born in Denmark in 1805, is still a popular writer today.

As a boy who was growing up in poverty, Hans had a hard life. His father, who was a shoemaker, could not even afford to make leather shoes for him, so he wore wooden shoes. His mother, who was unable to read or write, never encouraged him. His father died when he was eleven, so he went to work in a factory. Hans, who was dreaming of becoming an actor, could not work there for long. At age fourteen, he went to Copenhagen, which was the capital city of Denmark, to become an actor. Hans, who wanted his dream to come true, tried hard for three years, but he was not successful. The theater managers who saw him act said he was not a good actor, and they needed people with an education.

Hans Christian Andersen

Hans, who was feeling very disappointed, decided to go back to school. At age seventeen, he went to school with much younger students. Hans was tall, with big hands and feet, and he had a very big nose. The other students laughed at him. The lessons were difficult, but Hans, who was studying hard, got good grades. However, he was unhappy and wrote down his feelings. He later used these thoughts in his diary for his stories. *The Ugly Duckling*, which is a fairy tale about a baby duck with no friends, was really about himself.

Hans, who was like a child, was shy and sensitive, and he got hurt easily. He wanted to get married, but he was not successful. Andersen, who was getting disappointed, decided he would not marry.

At age thirty, he wrote his first fairy tales. The stories, which were thought to be too adult at first, were soon a great success. Andersen became famous, but he continued to be a shy and lonely man until he died at age seventy.

16 Practice

Complete the sentences with the past participle of verbs from the list.

drink   eat   fry   grow   mash   ripe   sell   serve   take

1. Most of the coffee _____ *grown* _____ in Brazil is exported.

2. The most popular hot beverage _____ by Americans is coffee.

3. Strawberries, bananas, tomatoes, and other fruits _____ in supermarkets are often unripe when they are picked.

4. Much of the fast food _____ by young people contains a lot of fat.

5. Hamburgers are eaten _____ on a bun.

6. Food _____ from the freezer must be defrosted before cooking.

7. Some people like potatoes _____ with butter; others like them

   _____ in oil.

8. Roquefort is a French cheese _____ in caves.

17 Your Turn

Work with a partner, a group, or alone. Write a fairy tale that you know (you can make changes to it) using reduced relative clauses. Read the fairy tale to the class.

Example:
Once upon a time, there was a little girl living in a forest . . .

_____

_____

_____

_____

_____

_____

_____

_____

REVIEW

1 Review (12a–12b, 12e–12f)

Underline the correct word in each sentence. Use formal English.

1. 1. John McDouall Stuart, (<u>who</u> / whom) was a British explorer, was the first man (<u>who</u> / whom) crossed Australia's center from the south coast to the Northern Territory.

2. Australia's vast unknown interior, (that / which) is very hot and dry, was a great challenge to explorers in the 1800s.

3. The natural forces (who / that) stopped him were extremely difficult to overcome.

4. The expeditions, for (that / which) he prepared for months, always ended in failure.

5. Other explorers (who / whom) Stuart met at the time had all failed, too.

6. They gave him advice, some of (whom / which) was useful, but most of (that / which) was not much help.

7. There was a shortage of water (who / that) he had to overcome, as well as hard, sharp grasses on (that / which) the horses and camels could not walk.

8. Natives, from (who / whom) he had to escape, chased him with their weapons.

9. Anyone (who / which) tried to cross Australia in those days had a very difficult time.

10. On his sixth expedition in 1862, Stuart was a man (who / whom) did not turn back.

11. He followed rivers and openings in the mountains, (that / which) made it possible for him to finally reach the sea near Darwin. He had crossed Australia for the first time!

12. No one knows the reason (why / which) Stuart stayed only one day. He returned almost a skeleton and had to be carried away. He died almost penniless at 51, but everyone remembers the important and difficult journey (who / that) he made.

Complete the sentences with the correct relative pronouns. Sometimes more than one pronoun is possible.

Some astronauts train in a laboratory _____*that*_____ is under water. Peggy

Whitson is an astronaut _____ has trained there. Where is the laboratory
                                    2

_____ she has trained? The lab, _____ is located three
          3   4

miles off the coast of Florida, is 62 feet below the surface of the ocean. This lab,

_____ is part of a National Aeronautical and Space Administration (NASA)
          5

program, is called Aquarius.

Is there a reason _____ astronauts train under water? Yes. Both space
                              6

and deep water are strange, difficult places for humans to live and work in,

_____ is why the lab is excellent for training astronauts. Whitson,
          7

_____ is only one of the astronauts _____ train in the lab,
          8   9

finds life under water similar to life in space.

The Aquarius crew, most of _____ are scientists and astronauts, stay in
                                        10

the lab for weeks. They live in an area _____ is similar in size to the space
                                                    11

station. The crew members, _____ leave the lab and go into the water,
                                        12

practice building and attaching structures to Aquarius, _____ is good
                                                                      13

practice for space walks. The crew members, _____ mission is also to
                                                            14

conduct experiments, work hard while they are in Aquarius.

Astronauts are not the only people _____ use Aquarius. This lab,
                                                15

_____ is so valuable to NASA, is actually owned by the National Oceanic
          16

and Atmospheric Association (NOAO). The people _____ work benefits the
                                                                17

most from the underwater lab are marine biologists.

Review (12a–12f)

Complete the sentences with the correct relative pronouns. Use informal English.

Rick: So this is the place _____*where*_____ you come to read.
1

Maria: That's right. The public library is the only place _____ it's quiet.
2

Rick: My sister, _____ I introduced to you last week, told me you've
3

           been here every night for a week.

Maria: Yes, the author _____ book I'm reading now is going to give a
4

           lecture at my school. I want to finish the book before he comes.

Rick: Do you mean the man _____ sailed around the world twice?
5

Maria: Yes. He sailed a boat _____ was only 25 feet long,
6

           _____ is small for the open ocean. He actually had two boats.
7

           One boat, _____ turned over while he was sailing around Cape Horn, sank.
8

Rick: I read about that. He lost his mast* in a violent storm, _____
9

           must have been a terrible experience. The Horn is an area _____
10

           waters are full of sunken ships. I know a woman _____ rolled
11

           over twice in her sailboat, _____ she was sailing there.
12

Maria: I'm fascinated by people _____ do adventurous things. My
13

           grandmother, _____ is 80 now, lived in Kenya for 10 years.
14

Rick: Really? How interesting. Oh, no! Someone took the book _____
15

           I put on this table. I need that book! My teacher, _____
16

           I expect to get an A from, asked me to get it for her.

Maria: The man _____ was standing here must have taken it.
17

Rick: Oh, no! The library card _____ Ms. Daniels gave me was in that book!
18

Maria: No, no. You gave me the card, _____ I then put in my pocket.
19

           You had a pile of books _____ you were about to drop.
20

Rick: You're right. Oh, I see the man _____ took my book. See? He's
21

           the one _____ the librarian is speaking to. I'll just go and get it
22

           back from him.

mast: A pole that holds up a sail on a sailboat

Find the errors and correct them.
Some errors are in punctuation.

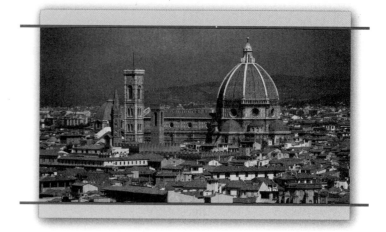

On the morning of November 4,

which

1966, ~~that~~ was a terrible day for art

lovers, it was raining very hard in

Italy. For many days, terrible rains

had fallen on Italy which cities are

filled with the world's greatest works of art. The Arno River, fill quickly, threatened to

flood. Just before dawn, the Arno River that flows through Florence overflowed its banks,

sending water into the countryside. The citizens of Florence which had been sleeping,

awakened to find their city under water. Florence who is a famous art center was under 14

feet of water and mud in some places. Thousands of art works many of whom were priceless

masterpieces were also under water. Suddenly Florence was a city who was a graveyard of

the world's finest art.

The Florentines that survived by climbing to their rooftops faced a terrible disaster. The

city that they loved was flooded. The greatest art works in the world many which had survived

for hundreds of years were buried in water and mud. But Florence is a city in whom there

are many art lovers.

On the morning after the flood, art students formed a human chain and pulled the art

works out of the water. Within 24 hours, people which restored paintings began arriving in

the city. It was a time that many people came together for a common cause—to save the

art work. This disaster from who the Florentines never expected to recover caught the

interest of people around the world. Donations came from everywhere. Experts worked tire-

lessly and much was saved. To be sure, many books and manuscripts who were very valuable

were lost to the flood, but many were rescued. Perhaps most important, the flood of 1966

taught lessons will not be forgotten. Experts developed new methods whom protect art-

works from natural disasters. People which worked on the art also developed new tech-

niques will help keep art safe for future generations.

A process is a series of steps that leads to an end. For example, a set of instructions on how to set up a computer is a process. Steps usually occur one after the other, but sometimes they happen at the same time. The order of the steps must be clear. If not, the process cannot be followed accurately. We can use time markers such as *first, then,* and *next* for the main steps. See page 260 for general writing guidelines. See page 261 for information on writing an essay.

Step 1. Discuss these process topics with a partner. Take notes on the important steps in the process.

a. How courtship works in your country

b. How you prepare for a wedding

c. How you prepare for a New Year's celebration

d. How you prepare for a religious holiday

Step 2. Choose one of the topics from Step 1, or use your own.

Step 3. Write your essay.

1. Choose three or four of the main steps for your topic. Write a paragraph for each step. Be sure to give details for each one. Use some adjective clauses in your paragraphs. Here is an example paragraph.

> Next, we prepare special food for this celebration. Dishes that are from an old tradition are prepared in a special way. For example, we always have a fish dish. The fish, which must be fresh, is boiled . . .

2. Write an introduction to the essay. Include a thesis statement stating the number of steps and briefly summarize them.

3. Write a conclusion. Your conclusion can summarize the information in the body and state why this process is important.

4. Write a title for your essay.

Step 4. Evaluate your essay.

Checklist

_____ Did you write an introduction, a paragraph for each step, and a conclusion?

_____ Did you write a title and put it in the right place?

_____ Did you present the order of the steps correctly and clearly?

_____ Would a reader who does not know the process understand it from your essay?

Step 5. Work with a partner or a teacher to edit your essay. Check spelling, vocabulary, and grammar.

Step 6. Write your final copy.

A **Choose the best answer, A, B, C, or D, to complete the sentence. Mark your answer by darkening the oval with the same letter. A—in an answer means that no word is needed to complete the sentence.**

1. That's the doctor _____ husband is an attorney.

   A. she's   Ⓐ Ⓑ Ⓒ Ⓓ
   B. who
   C. which
   D. whose

2. Tom, _____ was in our office yesterday, called me this morning.

   A. whose   Ⓐ Ⓑ Ⓒ Ⓓ
   B. who
   C. that
   D. which

3. Where is the person _____ I should give this?

   A. who   Ⓐ Ⓑ Ⓒ Ⓓ
   B. whom
   C. to whom
   D. to who

4. I remember the office _____ you worked when you first came to this city.

   A. which   Ⓐ Ⓑ Ⓒ Ⓓ
   B. where
   C. whom
   D. that

5. Do you remember Jo Brown, _____ worked with last year?

   A. which I   Ⓐ Ⓑ Ⓒ Ⓓ
   B. I
   C. who I
   D. who

6. Jack found the information _____ was looking for on the Internet.

   A. he   Ⓐ Ⓑ Ⓒ Ⓓ
   B. who
   C. for which
   D. that

7. The person _____ the award was given will appear on television tonight.

   A. whom   Ⓐ Ⓑ Ⓒ Ⓓ
   B. who
   C. to whom
   D. who to

8. I don't like the book _____ our teacher chose for us.

   A. —   Ⓐ Ⓑ Ⓒ Ⓓ
   B. whom
   C. what
   D. who

9. I have applied to two universities, _____ are in this city.

   A. both which   Ⓐ Ⓑ Ⓒ Ⓓ
   B. both of which
   C. of which
   D. both of whom

10. Prague, _____ capital of the Czech Republic, is a beautiful city.

    A. that is the   Ⓐ Ⓑ Ⓒ Ⓓ
    B. the
    C. where
    D. is being

B Find the underlined word or phrase, A, B, C, or D, that is incorrect. Mark your answer by darkening the oval with the same letter.

1. I went <u>to visit</u> a friend <u>his</u> father is the
   A B
   <u>president</u> of <u>your brother's</u> college.
   C D

   Ⓐ Ⓑ Ⓒ Ⓓ

2. I remember <u>the hotel</u> <u>for which</u> we <u>stayed</u>
   A B C
   at <u>that</u> your friend owned.
   D

   Ⓐ Ⓑ Ⓒ Ⓓ

3. We enjoyed <u>watching</u> the show <u>that</u> you
   A B
   <u>told us</u> <u>about it</u>.
   C D

   Ⓐ Ⓑ Ⓒ Ⓓ

4. An <u>author</u> <u>who's</u> books <u>I like</u> a lot <u>is</u>
   A B C D
   Stephen King.

   Ⓐ Ⓑ Ⓒ Ⓓ

5. <u>His collection</u> of paintings, <u>most of them</u>
   A B
   <u>are</u> from the twentieth century, <u>is</u> famous.
   C D

   Ⓐ Ⓑ Ⓒ Ⓓ

6. My brother, <u>who his</u> company <u>makes</u> toys,
   A B
   <u>has moved</u> to <u>another city</u>.
   C D

   Ⓐ Ⓑ Ⓒ Ⓓ

7. <u>The organization</u>, <u>it</u> <u>having many members</u>,
   A B C
   <u>is</u> famous throughout the world.
   D

   Ⓐ Ⓑ Ⓒ Ⓓ

8. <u>Do you</u> know <u>the name</u> of <u>the teacher is</u>
   A B C
   <u>standing</u> by the window?
   D

   Ⓐ Ⓑ Ⓒ Ⓓ

9. All of the facts <u>what</u> <u>I have told</u> you <u>are</u>
   A B C
   true and <u>can be found</u> in this book.
   D

   Ⓐ Ⓑ Ⓒ Ⓓ

10. <u>This course</u>, <u>which</u> I <u>had</u> to buy this
    A B C
    book, <u>will be</u> very useful for me.
    D

    Ⓐ Ⓑ Ⓒ Ⓓ

UNIT 13

ADVERB CLAUSES

13a Adverb Clauses of Time

Ricky listens to music **while he does his homework.**

1. There are many kinds of adverb clauses. We recognize them by their special clause markers* (conjunctions), for example, *when, as soon as, where, although,* and *because.*

2. Adverb clauses of time and place work like adverbs. They tell when and where something happens.

    I do my homework **as soon as I come home from school.**
    While I do my homework, I listen to music.

3. An adverb clause of time is a dependent clause. It must be used with a main clause. When an adverb clause comes at the beginning of a sentence, we put a comma after it. We do not use a comma when it comes at the end.

Clause Marker	Use	Examples
as while when whenever	To say that things happen at the same time. *Whenever* has the additional meaning of "every time."	**As** I was driving down the street, I saw Susan. I watch television **while** I'm having breakfast. They were sleeping **when** they saw the bear.
		I order the fish **whenever** I go to that restaurant.
when** before after	To say that things happen one after another.	**When** he finished his test, he left the room. The show had begun **before** we arrived. **After** he finished his course, he found a job.

  *See Page 253 for more information on adverb clause markers.
  **We can use *when* instead of *while, as, before,* and *after* if the order of events is clear from other information in the sentence.

    When/While/As I was writing my essay, I had a brilliant idea.
    The movie had begun when/before we arrived.
    When/after he finished his degree, he quickly found a job.

Clause Marker	Use	Examples
as soon as once	To say that one thing happens quickly after another.	Please feed the dog **as soon as** you get home. **Once** he got home, he fed the dog.
the first time the next time the last time	To say which of several occurrences of something that we are talking about.	**The first time** I ate sushi, I hated it. **The next time** I ate it, I liked it a little bit. **The last time** I ate it, I ate all of it.
until	To say that something continues up to the time when something else happens.	You must stay in class **until** you finish your essay.
as long as*	To say that something continues to the end of something else.	I will dance **as long as** the band plays. (When the band stops playing, I will stop dancing.)
by the time	To say that something happens no later than the time when something else happens.	I will have finished my work **by the time** you come home.
since	To say that something happens between a point in the past and the present.	I've seen a lot of the city **since** I came here.

*We can also say *so long as*.

1 Practice

A. Read about Helen Thayer's life.

Helen Thayer was the first woman to walk to the North Pole alone and unaided. She walked and skied for 27 days, pulling a 160-pound sled for 364 miles. She had no help from aircraft, dog teams, or snowmobiles. Helen was born in New Zealand. Here are some facts about her life:

B. Match the sentences to learn more about Helen Thayer.

_b_   **1.** She was attacked by polar bears.

_____   **2.** She was resting at night.

_____   **3.** She knew she would not give up.

_____   **4.** She returned home.

_____   **5.** She returned from her trip.

a. She achieved her goal.

b. Her dog Charlie protected her.

c. She has traveled all over the world, giving talks about her amazing experiences.

d. She wrote a book, *Polar Dream,* about her amazing adventure.

e. She talked to Charlie about her thoughts and plans.

C. Using the clause markers in parentheses, combine the pairs of sentences from part B.

1. (when) _When she was attacked by polar bears, her dog Charlie protected her._

2. (while) _____

_____

3. (until) _____

_____

4. (as soon as) _____

_____

5. (since) _____

_____

2 | What Do You Think?

What is your opinion of Helen Thayer's achievement? Which fact do you find most surprising or interesting?

3 | Your Turn

Work with a partrner. Tell your partner about a personal goal that you have achieved. What did you do before? What did you do after? How has your life changed since you achieved that goal?

Example:
I achieved a goal when I got my drivers license. After I got it, I was able to drive myself to school, and I became a lot more independent.

13b Adverb Clauses of Reason and Result

Mona has a headache **because she has too much to do.**

1. There are several kinds of sentences that express a reason or a result. In these examples, notice that both the result and the reason can be in a main clause or an adverb clause.

   Result (main clause)
   I felt tired in the morning

   Reason (adverb clause)
   because I had gone to bed very late.

   Reason (main clause)
   I had gone to bed very late,

   Result (adverb clause)
   so I felt tired in the morning.

2. We use these clause markers to introduce clauses of reason.

   as   because   since   so

   Clauses with *because, as,* and *since* can go at the beginning or end of the sentence. We put a comma after the clause if it comes at the beginning. Result clauses with *so* must go at the end of the sentence. We put a comma in front of them.

   The children shouldn't have any ice cream now **because they're going to have dinner in half an hour.**
   As/Since the weather is bad, we shouldn't go out tonight.
   I got up very early, **so I needed another cup of coffee.**

   Do not confuse *because* with *because of.* Both show reasons, but *because of* is followed by a noun, not a subject and a verb.

   Because it was raining, we stayed home.
   Because of the rain, we stayed home.

Since and *as* mean about the same thing as *because,* but they suggest a meaning like "It is a fact that . . . " or "It is true that . . . "

Remember, *since* is also a time clause marker. See page 171.

3. We can use *so* + adjective/adverb + *that* or *such* + adjective + noun + *that* to show a result. They have the same meaning.

>   The sandwich was **so** tasty **that** I had another one.
>   It was **such** a tasty sandwich **that** I had another one.

We can also use *such* + a noun with or without an adjective. In informal English, we can omit the *that* clause.

>   It was **such** a terrible disaster (that it was on the evening news).
>   It was **such** a disaster (that it was on the evening news).

When we speak, we often omit *that*.

>   It was **such** tasty soup (that) I had another bowl.
>   The movie was **so** good (that) I saw it three times.

4. There are other clause markers that introduce clauses of result. These markers introduce main clauses, not dependent clauses, so their punctuation is different. Clauses with these markers always go at the end of the sentence. Sometimes they can also be a separate sentence.

Main Clause (Reason)	Clause Marker	Main Clause (Result)
Our teacher was sick;	**as a result,**	our class was canceled.
I don't know much about computers;	**therefore,**	I can't help you.
The weather is very severe;	**consequently,**	all flights will be delayed.

We can punctuate the long clause markers *as a result, therefore,* and *consequently* in two ways. We can put a semicolon before the clause marker and a comma after it, or we can write two sentences with a comma after the clause marker.

>   One Sentence: I don't know much about computers; **therefore,** I can't help you.
>   Two Sentences: I don't know much about computers. **Therefore,** I can't help you.

We can use *and* before these clause markers. In these cases, we use a comma between the two clauses.

>   He was very qualified, **and so** he got the job.
>   Our teacher was sick, **and as a result** our class was canceled.

4 Practice

Complete the sentences with *so* or *because*. Add commas where necessary.

1. On Monday, I got up early _____*because*_____ I had an important meeting.

2. I had gone to bed late _____ I felt tired when I got up.

3. I needed more energy _____ I drank some coffee.

4. I took an umbrella _____ it was raining.

5. It was an important interview _____ I wore my best suit.

6. I was feeling rather nervous _____ my boss was going to be there.

7. There was a lot of traffic _____ my bus was late.

8. My papers got mixed up _____ I dropped my briefcase.

9. My suit got mud on it _____ I was standing too near the cars, and it was raining.

10. I finally arrived in a complete mess. I was one hour late. The office was empty. I found a note which said, "Punctuality is very important to this company _____ you are fired."

5 Practice

Rewrite each of the sentences in two ways, once using *so . . . that* and once using *such a/an . . . that*.

Esmeralda was lost in the forest. She wandered through the trees all day until she came to a small house.

1. The door to the house was very small. She had to stoop down to go in.

   The house was so small that she had to stoop down to go in.

   It was such a small house that she had to stoop down to go in.

2. The chairs and tables were very delicate. She was afraid to touch them.

   _____

   _____

3. A delicious cake was on the kitchen table. She ate three slices.

   _____

   _____

4. The house was very beautiful. She felt like she wanted to stay there forever.

_____

_____

5. The bed was very soft. She couldn't help lying down.

_____

_____

6. She heard some soft music. She fell asleep immediately.

_____

_____

7. She had a very peaceful dream. She didn't want to wake up.

_____

_____

8. She heard a loud noise. She woke up suddenly.

_____

_____

9. The moon was very bright. She could see outside as though it were day.

_____

_____

6 What Do You Think?

Finish the story in your own words.

7 Your Turn

Tell a partner about something that was good, horrible, or difficult for you. Use an idea from the list or one of your own.

Example:
I once saw a movie that was so good that I went to see it three times. It was about people in a small mountain village.

a movie
something to eat
a grammar point

13c Adverb Clauses of Purpose

Maria writes everything down
so that she can remember it.

1. We use clauses of purpose to answer the questions *what for?* and *for what
    purpose?* We use the clause markers *so that* or *in order that** to introduce adverb
    clauses of purpose. In speech, we can omit *that* when we use *so that*.

    I'm saving money **so (that)** I can buy a car.
    We saved a lot of money **in order that** we could take a long vacation.

2. We can introduce a phrase (not a clause) of purpose with *in order to* + a base verb.

    I'm saving money **in order to** buy a car.

3. We often use *so that* with *can, can't, will,* or *won't* for the present or future, and
    could, couldn't, would, or *wouldn't* for the past. We sometimes, but not often, use
    may or *might* in place of *can* or *could*.

    He writes down everything **so (that)** he **can** remember it.
    She gets up early **so (that)** she **won't** be late.
    He wrote down everything **so (that)** he **could** remember it.
    She got up early **so (that)** she **wouldn't** be late.
    He wrote it down **so that** he **might** remember it.

    *In order that is rare.

8 | Practice

Complete the sentences with *so that* to show purpose or *therefore* to show result. Add commas, semicolons, periods, and capital letters where necessary.

Joanna wanted to go to the United States <u> so that </u> she could improve her
1

English. She enrolled in an English program at a university _____ she could learn
2

quickly. She lived with her uncle and aunt, who wanted to speak their language with her

_____ she couldn't practice English at home. At first, her English wasn't very good.
3

_____ she had to work hard. She learned to keep a notebook with her at all times
4

_____ she could write down new idioms and expressions that she heard. Also, she
5

joined some clubs at the university. Many American students became her friends

_____ she was able to practice with them.
6

After six months, her English was very good. _____ she decided to return
7

home. She bought a computer _____ she could stay in touch with her American
8

friends. Now she is looking for a job in tourism _____ she will be able to use her
9

English at work.

9 | Your Turn

Talk about yourself with a partner. Use *so that* for purpose and *so* or *therefore* for result. Use ideas from the list or your own.

Example:
I watch a lot of American movies so that I can improve my English.
It's important for me to have good English, so I practice as much as possible.
OR It's important for me to have good English; therefore, I practice as much as possible.

speak good English
improve my vocabulary/grammar
make friends
be successful
get married
travel a lot

13d Adverb Clauses of Contrast

Even though Tony apologized, Anne is still angry with him.

1. We use adverb clauses of contrast to show that two ideas differ, often in an unexpected or unusual way. We introduce them with the following clause markers.

   although   even though   though   whereas   while

   > **Although** there was a snowstorm, all the trains were on time.
   > **Even though** there was a snowstorm, all the trains were on time.
   > **Though** there was a snowstorm, all the trains were on time.

2. *Even though* is more emphatic than *although*. *Though* is not as formal as *even though* or *although*.

3. In informal English, we can also use *though* to mean "however." In this case, it often comes at the end of a sentence. There is often a comma before it in writing.

   > It is very cold outside. It's nice and warm in here, **though**.
   > = It's very cold outside; however, it's nice and warm in here.

4. We can also use *while* and *whereas* to introduce contrast between two ideas.

   > Jim has dark hair, **while** his brother has light hair.
   > Jim has dark hair, **whereas** his brother has light hair.

5. We can also show contrast between two ideas by using the transitional main clause markers *however* or *nevertheless*. Note the position and punctuation with *however* and *nevertheless*.

   > I enjoy living in the city; **however,** the cost of living is quite high.
   > I enjoy living in the city. **However,** the cost of living is quite high.

   > I enjoy living in the city; **nevertheless,** I'm going to move to the suburbs soon.
   > I enjoy living in the city. **Nevertheless,** I'm going to move to the suburbs soon.

10 Practice

Match the clauses and then combine them into sentences using *although, even though, while,* or *whereas.* Use correct punctuation.

_f_	**1.** Samuel is rich	**a.** he doesn't know what to spend it on
_____	**2.** Samuel has a lot of "friends"	**b.** he doesn't like his job
_____	**3.** Samuel works very hard	**c.** none of them would help him if he were in trouble
_____	**4.** Samuel has a lot of money	
_____	**5.** A lot of people want to meet him	**d.** none of them feels like home
		e. he doesn't want to meet them
_____	**6.** Samuel has several houses	**f.** he isn't happy

1. _Although Samuel is rich, he isn't happy._

2. _____

3. _____

4. _____

5. _____

6. _____

11 Practice

Rewrite four of the sentences from Practice 11 using *however* or *nevertheless.* Use correct punctuation.

1. _Samuel is rich; however, he is unhappy._

2. _____

3. _____

4. _____

13e Adverb Clauses of Condition

Claudia's parents said they'd buy her
a car **only if she graduated.**

1. Clauses of condition show that one thing depends on another. We use these
   markers to introduce clauses of condition.

even if	in case	unless
if	only if	whether or not

2. *If* clauses are adverb clauses of condition. The *if* clause contains the condition
   and the main clause contains the result. We use the simple present tense in the
   if clause, even if the main clause refers to the future.

   > **If** I feel better tomorrow, I'll go to class.
   > I'll stay in bed **if** I don't go to class.

3. We use *whether or not* to say that a situation will not be affected by one thing or
   another. *Even if* is close in meaning to *whether or not*. It means that no matter
   what the condition, the result will not change.

   > **Whether or not** I feel well tomorrow, I'm going to school.
   > OR **Whether** I feel well **or not** tomorrow, I'm going to school.
   > **Even if** I am sick tomorrow, I'm going to school.
   > (I don't care if I am sick. It doesn't matter. I'm going to school tomorrow.)

4. We use *unless* to mean "if . . . not."

   > **Unless** I feel well, I won't go to school.
   > (If I don't feel well, I won't go to school.)

   > You can't see the doctor **unless** you have an appointment.
   > (You can't see the doctor if you don't have an appointment.)

We often use *unless* in threats and warnings.

> You can't go out **unless** you finish your homework.
> **Unless** you have an emergency, you must attend class.

5. We use *only if* to mean there is only one condition for a certain result.

> My parents will buy me a new computer **only if** I pass this class.
> (If I don't pass this class, they won't buy me a computer.)

When we put *only if* at the beginning of a sentence, we must invert the subject and the verb.

> **Only if** I pass this class will my parents buy me a computer.

6. We use *in case* to talk about things we do because we think something else might happen.

> I'll make some extra food **in case** John wants to stay for dinner.
> (I will make some extra food now. Then if John wants to stay, there will be enough food for him, too. If he doesn't want to stay for dinner, it doesn't matter.)

See Unit 14 for more information on clauses of conditon.

12 Practice

Write sentences that express rules for using computers in the library. Match the halves of the following sentences using adverbial clause markers from the list. Use each marker only once (but more than one may be possible for some answers).

| even if | in case | unless |
| if | only if | whether |

___a___ **1.** You may not use the computer

         2. Children under six may use the computer

         3. You need to get a new password

         4. Ask a librarian for assistance

         5. The maximum time per person is one hour

         6. You may use the computer for the maximum time

a. you have already registered with the library

b. you can't log on to the Internet

c. they are accompanied by an adult

d. another student is waiting

e. other students are waiting or not

f. you forget your old one

1. _You may not use the computer unless you have already_
   registered with the library.

2. _____

   _____

3. _____

   _____

4. _____

   _____

5. _____

   _____

6. _____

   _____

13 Your Turn

Write rules for one of the following situations, or use your own idea. Use adverb clauses of condition in your rules.

borrowing books from your school or public library
using your local sports center or swimming pool
using the kitchen in an apartment shared by several students

_____

_____

_____

_____

_____

_____

_____

13f Reduced Adverb Clauses

Since starting class, I have made a lot of friends.

1. We can reduce an adverb clause to a modifying adverb phrase in the same way we reduce adjective clauses to adjective phrases. An adverb phrase does not have a subject or a verb. It consists of a present or past participle and an adverb clause time marker. The present participle replaces verbs in the active voice, and the past participle replaces verbs in the passive voice.

   Adverb Clause: **Before I came** to the United States, I took some English classes.
   Adverb Phrase: **Before coming** to the United States, I took some English classes.

   Adverb Clause: The Internet was for the use of university and government scientists **when it was originally invented.**
   Adverb Phrase: **When originally invented,** the Internet was for the use of university and government scientists.

   We can use modifying adverb phrases with verbs of any tense in the main clause.

   Before going to Korea, I **will take** some Korean classes. (main verb is future)
   When completed, these products **sell** around the world. (main verb is present)

2. The modifying adverb phrase can come before or after the main clause. We use a comma after the adverb phrase when it comes at the beginning of a sentence.

   Since starting this class, she has made a lot of friends.
   She has made a lot of friends **since starting** this class.

3. We can only change an adverb clause to an adverb phrase when the subject of the main clause and the adverb clause are the same.

    Adverb Clause: While **I** was traveling across Europe, **I** noticed the differences in architecture.
    Adverb Phrase: While traveling across Europe, I noticed the differences in architecture.

    Adverb Clause: While **I** was traveling across Europe, the **differences** in architecture became very clear.
    Adverb Phrase: (No reduction possible)

We can sometimes omit *while* and still keep the meaning "at the same time."

    Traveling across Europe, I noticed the differences in architecture.

4. We do not use *because* in an adverb phrase. We omit *because* and use only the *-ing* phrase. This gives the same meaning as *because*.

    Because he wanted to pass the class, he studied very hard.
    Wanting to pass the class, he studied very hard.

5. We sometimes use *upon* or *on* in place of *when* in an adverb phrase. The meaning is the same.

    Adverb Clause: **When we entered** the house, we took off our shoes.
    Adverb Phrase: **Upon entering** the house, we took off our shoes.
    Adverb Phrase: **On entering** the house, we took off our shoes.

14 Practice

Complete the sentences about Julia's study routine with reduced adverb clauses. Some sentences require an adverb from the list; others do not. Some sentences require present participles; some require past participles.

after	once	when
before	since	while

    Julia is a very organized person, and she has a definite study routine. She gets up at 6:00

every morning and goes running for 30 minutes (begin) _____*before beginning*_____
                                                          1

work. (run) _____, she thinks about the day ahead and plans
                            2

her schedule. (come back) _____ from her run, she takes
                                      3

a shower and eats breakfast. Then she sets herself a goal for each part of her day.

(set) _____ her goals, she also estimates
                        4
how long each one will take and which ones are most important.

(complete) _____, her goals are checked
                        5
off on a calendar above her desk. This helps her to track her progress.

(hope) _____ to get high grades in her courses .
                        6
this semester, she has set herself a strict schedule. She studies for four hours every

morning. She sometimes listens to music (study) _____.
                                                                        7
(eat) _____ lunch, she goes to classes or to the
                        8
library to do research. (start) _____ to use this
                                                        9
study schedule, she has found that her grades have improved, and she is able to

get her work completed on time. (check) _____ by her
                                                                10
teacher, her assignments are organized in a special folder according to date and topic.

(file) _____ neatly, her work will be easier to find when she
                        11
needs to review for her exams.

15 Practice

Read the sentences. Can they be reduced or not? Write Y (for _yes_) or N (for _no_) next to each one. If the sentence can be reduced, rewrite it.

___Y___ **1.** After she finishes an assignment, Julia checks her work carefully.

After finishing an assignment, Julia checks her work carefully.

_____ **2.** When her work is completed, Julia's friends can call her up on the phone.

_____

     3. Since she started her new schedule, Julia has been much happier.

     4. When the instructor gives a new assignment, Julia starts work on it immediately.

     5. While the instructor is handing out the grades, Julia feels very anxious.

     6. Julia knows that she must stay healthy, so she runs every day and eats lots of fruit.

     7. Before she returns home, she goes to the coffee shop with her friends.

     8. When Julia gets a good grade, her parents are very pleased.

16 Your Turn

Tell a partner about your study or work routine. Ask and answer questions like the following, or use your own ideas.

Example:
I feel very tired in the morning, so after getting up, I take a shower. While showering, I listen to loud music on the radio. That helps me wake up . . .

What do you do before starting work/school?
What do you do while working/studying?
What do you do after finishing work/school?

REVIEW

1 Review (13a–13b, 13d–13e)

Underline the correct words.

Paul Gaugin was born in Paris, (<u>but</u> / even though) he spent part of his childhood in
1
Peru before his family returned to France. (Even though / While) a young man, he worked
2
as a sailor; (whereas / however), he eventually settled down and got married. (While as /
3   4
While) he was married, he worked as a stockbroker and had five children. (As / Although)
                                                                                        5
time went by, Gaugin took up painting as a hobby. (After / Before) a few years, he realized
                                                     6
that he wasn't happy (in case / unless) he was painting. (As / When) he was 35, he quit
                      7   8
his job and started to paint full time; (although / however), he could not make enough
                                          9
money to support his family. (Even though / Because) his wife loved him, she felt she had
                              10
to leave. She took the children to her family in Denmark (as / so) they could have food and
                                                          11
clothes. (Whereas / Although) they had been happy for a time, Gaugin and his wife never
         12
lived together again.

(Because / While) Gaugin had a unique style of painting, he had difficulty selling his
13
work; (nevertheless / consequently), he refused to give up. He was painting in large shapes
        14
and bright colors, (whereas / because) other artists were painting the old way, with small
                    15
detail and dark colors. There were a few other artists, such as Vincent Van Gogh, who were
trying new things, (so that / but) they weren't selling their works either; (nevertheless /
                   16   17
consequently), they were very poor.

Gaugin got tired of it all, (so / when) in 1891 he decided to go to the island of Tahiti in
                            18
the South Pacific. (After/ While) landing there, he moved into a grass hut and started to
                   19
paint. Gaugin went back to France in 1893. He hoped to sell his paintings; (however /
                                                                                    20
although), the trip was not a success. Two years later, Gaugin went back to Tahiti—never
to return home. In 1901, he went to the Marquesas Islands where he died penniless and
alone. Like Van Gogh, he was considered a failure as an artist; (as a result / nevertheless),
                                                                                 21
after their deaths they became famous. Today their paintings sell for millions of dollars.

Read this Greek myth and complete the sentences using the adverbial clause markers from the list. Sometimes there is more than one correct answer. Add commas and semicolons where necessary.

after	because	even though	so
although	but	however	therefore
as	by the time	if only	unless
as soon as	consequently	since	when

Pyramus and Thisbe were in love, _____so_____ they wanted to be together.
1

_____ they were neighbors, they could never meet.
2

_____ their parents disliked each other, they forbade Pyramus and
3

Thisbe to see one another. _____ there was a space in the wall between
4

their houses, _____ the young lovers were able to whisper to each
5

other. _____ their parents forbade it, they wanted very much to be
6

together. _____ they were so much in love, this was too much to endure.
7

_____ a while, Pyramus came up with a plan. They couldn't marry
8

_____ they ran away. They agreed to meet outside the city. Thisbe
9

arrived at the place under a mulberry tree* _____ a lion with bloody
10

jaws frightened her away. _____ she left, the lion found her scarf
11

and ripped it up. _____ Pyramus came along, he found the bloody
12

scarf and the lion's footprints. He thought Thisbe had been killed. _____
13

he had arrived sooner, he could have saved her! _____ he could not
14

accept the thought of living without Thisbe, he took his sword and stabbed it into his

body. _____ the blood spurted** upward, it dyed the white mulberries red.
15

_____ Thisbe returned, her lover was dying.
16

_____ she took the sword and killed herself. The parents saw how
17

much their children had loved each other _____ they buried them in
18

a single urn.*** _____ that time, the mulberry tree has produced
19

red berries.

* *mulberry:* A tree that bears a red fruit

** *spurted:* (of a liquid) to shoot upward with force

*** *urn:* a kind of vase

A. Match the clauses.

although	even though	so that
because	however	whereas
but	nevertheless	
even if	so	

___i___ 1. Jeff is starting a new job today   a. a friend offered to drive him

_____ 2. He set his alarm clock   b. it is difficult at first

_____ 3. He changed his clothes three times before leaving home   c. he would wake up on time

_____ 4. Jeff wanted to drive his car today   d. he had chosen a suit the night before

_____ 5. He's going to take the bus today   e. he has never worked in an office

_____ 6. He will usually take the bus   f. he hasn't met any of his coworkers

_____ 7. He thinks he's well prepared for a job as a computer programmer   g. he wants to save money on gas

_____ 8. Jeff had several jobs while he was in school   h. he's afraid they'll ask him something he doesn't know

_____ 9. Jeff has met his new boss   i. he's a little nervous

_____ 10. He is determined to succeed in this job   j. it is in the shop for repairs

B. Combine the clauses in Part A using adverbial markers from the list. Sometimes more than one marker is possible.

1. _Jeff is starting a new job today, so he's a little nervous._

2. _____

3. _____

4. _____

5. _____

6. _____

7. _____

8. _____

9. _____

10. _____

4 Review (13a, 13c–13f)

Find the errors in clause markers and correct them. Watch for missing punctuation.

~~As soon as~~ *As* more and more people try cross-country, or Nordic, skiing, it is becoming more popular than ever. There are several reasons why. In order ski downhill or snowboard, you must have deep snow where to do cross-country skiing you need only a few inches of snow on the ground. While you do downhill skiing you need to go to a special area and take lifts to the top of the mountain, nevertheless when do cross-country skiing, you can use any field or forest. You don't need to buy lift tickets to ski along a forest trail because cross-country skiing doesn't cost very much to do.

Because of you're not rushing down a hill at a high speed Nordic skiing is safe and easy to learn. It's good for you too. Since you're enjoying your winter surroundings, you're also getting a good physical workout. While you're ready to go cross-country skiing it's easy to find good cross-country routes. Even there's no snow where you live most mountain ski areas have miles and miles of trails.

Since it became a popular sport cross-country skiing was often the only way people could travel in snow country. In cold areas of the north, people couldn't go anywhere though they strapped on their skis. Because some people still cross-country ski out of necessity, most people do it for fun. Before go cross-country skiing, you probably should take a lesson. It may seem hard at first since most instructors say that people are usually gliding along after only a few hours.

When we compare, we look at the similarities between two things. When we contrast, we look at their differences. See page 260 for general writing guidelines. See page 261 for information on writing an essay.

Step 1. Choose a topic from the list below. Take notes on the similarities or differences between the two things. Decide whether you want to write an essay of comparison or an essay of contrast.

1. life in the country and life in the city

2. transportation now and transportation twenty years ago

3. owning a car or travel by public transportation

4. studying in a foreign country or study in your country

Transportation Now and 20 Years Ago

Similarities
most people drive cars
air travel for long distance
few areas have mass transit

Differences
some cars are more efficient now
air travel less comfortable then
some cars run on electricity now

Step 2. Choose two or three points of comparison or contrast.

Step 3. Write your essay. Use some of the words and phrases of comparison and contrast on page 463. Write a title for your essay. Organize your essay like this.

1. Introduction: State your topic and include a thesis statement that explains what you are going to say.

2. Body: Write a paragraph on each of the points you chose in Step 2.

3. Conclusion: Summarize your points and restate your thesis statement.

Step 4. Evaluate your essay.

Checklist

_____ Did you write an introduction with a thesis statement, one paragraph for each point of comparison or contrast, and a conclusion?

_____ Do your paragraphs support your thesis statement?

_____ Did you use some words and phrases of comparison or contrast?

Step 5. Work with a partner or a teacher to edit your essay. Check spelling, vocabulary, and grammar.

Step 6. Write your final copy.

A   Choose the best answer, A, B, C, or D, to complete the sentence. Mark your answer by darkening the oval with the same letter.

1. _____ she arrives, she will check in to a hotel.

   A. As soon as   (A) (B) (C) (D)
   B. It is when
   C. Since
   D. As

2. _____ she was late, she didn't hurry.

   A. For   (A) (B) (C) (D)
   B. Nevertheless
   C. However
   D. Although

3. The movie was so good _____ saw it three times.

   A. although I   (A) (B) (C) (D)
   B. that I
   C. for I
   D. because I

4. We didn't go on a picnic _____ it was raining.

   A. although   (A) (B) (C) (D)
   B. because of
   C. because
   D. as a result

5. She went to the library _____ return a book.

   A. in order to   (A) (B) (C) (D)
   B. so to
   C. because
   D. so that to

6. It was _____ a difficult poem that nobody in class understood it.

   A. so   (A) (B) (C) (D)
   B. too
   C. such
   D. that

7. Take some food with you _____ you get hungry on the way.

   A. in case   (A) (B) (C) (D)
   B. unless
   C. even if
   D. while

8. You should see a doctor _____ you don't feel well.

   A. unless   (A) (B) (C) (D)
   B. if
   C. in order to
   D. because of

9. _____ the best qualifications, she got the job.

   A. Because having   (A) (B) (C) (D)
   B. Because she having
   C. Having
   D. Because having

10. _____ sitting on a train, he had an idea.

   A. While   (A) (B) (C) (D)
   B. While he
   C. He was
   D. While was

B Find the underlined word or phrase, A, B, C, or D, that is incorrect. Mark your answer by darkening the oval with the same letter.

1. <u>Even</u> he has <u>a number of</u> relatives <u>who</u>
   A   B   C

   live close by, he never visits <u>them</u>.
                             D

   Ⓐ Ⓑ Ⓒ Ⓓ

2. She has <u>so</u> a good memory <u>that</u> she can
          A   B

   remember a <u>person's</u> exact words <u>even</u> a
               C   D

   week later.

   Ⓐ Ⓑ Ⓒ Ⓓ

3. He repeated <u>all</u> the new <u>vocabulary</u>
              A   B

   <u>in order</u> remember <u>it</u>.
   C   D

   Ⓐ Ⓑ Ⓒ Ⓓ

4. <u>Why don't we</u> close all the windows <u>case</u>
   A   B

   <u>it rains</u> <u>while</u> we are not home?
   C   D

   Ⓐ Ⓑ Ⓒ Ⓓ

5. <u>She is</u> very <u>organized</u> at work; <u>therefore,</u>
    B   B   C

   her apartment is very <u>messy</u>.
                     D

   Ⓐ Ⓑ Ⓒ Ⓓ

6. <u>Because working</u> from home, Ken <u>had</u>
   A   B

   <u>little</u> <u>contact</u> with people.
   C   D

   Ⓐ Ⓑ Ⓒ Ⓓ

7. She called her mother <u>soon as</u> <u>she</u> heard
                      A   B

   <u>she</u> <u>had passed</u> the test.
   C   D

   Ⓐ Ⓑ Ⓒ Ⓓ

8. Whether <u>or not</u> <u>I pass</u> the test tomorrow,
           A   B

   I <u>will call</u> you <u>or not</u>.
     C   D

   Ⓐ Ⓑ Ⓒ Ⓓ

9. <u>I'll take</u> my umbrella with me now <u>if</u> it
   A   B

   <u>rains</u> <u>later</u>.
   C   D

   Ⓐ Ⓑ Ⓒ Ⓓ

10. Only if <u>I</u> <u>found</u> a job here <u>I would</u> <u>move</u>
             A   B   C   D

    to this city.

UNIT 14

CONDITIONAL SENTENCES

14a Real Conditional Sentences in the Present and Future

Form

If you **water** a plant, it **grows.**

1. We use two clauses in a conditional sentence, a dependent *if* clause and a main clause. The *if* clause states a condition, and the main clause states a result.

2. The *if* clause can come before or after the main clause with no change in meaning. If the *if* clause comes first, we put a comma after it.

3. A sentence that expresses a real condition has a present tense verb in the *if* clause, and a present or future verb in the main clause.

4. *If* clauses can go at the beginning or the end of a sentence. We put a comma after the *if* clause if it comes first.

> **If you water a plant,** it grows.
> A plant grows **if you water it.**

IF CLAUSE			MAIN CLAUSE		
Subject	Present Tense Verb		Subject	Present or Future Tense Verb	
If you	**water**	a plant,	it	**grows.**	
If it	**rains**	tomorrow,	we	**will go**	to a movie.

Function

1. We use the present real conditional (present tense in the main clause) to say that something always happens in a specific situation.

> If I **eat** too much, I **don't** feel well.

2. We use the present real conditional to talk about a general fact that is always true.

> If you **heat** butter, it **melts.**

3. We use the future real conditional (future tense in the main clause) to talk about something that may possibly happen in the future.

> If it **rains**, we **will go** to a movie. (It may rain, or it may not. But if it does, we will go to a movie.)

> If my parents **come** to visit me this summer, **I'm going to take** them to New York.

4. We can also use *should* after *if* when we are less sure of something.

> If I **see** Tony, I'll tell him. (Perhaps I will see Tony.)
> If I **should see** Tony, I'll tell him. (I am less sure I will see Tony.)

5. We can also use the imperative in the main clause of a future conditional sentence.

> If you see Tony, **tell** him to wait.
> If the phone rings, please **pick** it **up**.

---

1 Practice

With a partner, read the proverbs and decide what they mean. Then rewrite the proverbs using *if* sentences in the present tense. (Note: *He who . . .* is a way of starting a proverb. It means "a person who . . .")

1. Don't cry over spilt milk. (*spilt* = spilled)

   If you make a mistake, there is no point in crying about it.

2. Look before you leap. (*leap* = jump)

   _____

3. Many hands make light work. (*light* = easy)

   _____

4. Where there's smoke, there's fire.

   _____

5. An apple a day keeps the doctor away.

   _____

6. It never rains, but it pours. (= Every time it rains, it pours.)

   _____

7. Fish and guests smell after three days.

   _____

8. First things first. (First things come first.)

_____

9. Nothing ventured, nothing gained. (*ventured* = risked, tried)

_____

10. He who hesitates is lost.

_____

11. He who pays the piper calls the tune. (a piper plays a flute-like instrument; *calls the tune* = decides which song will be played)

_____

12. He who laughs last laughs best.

_____

2 Practice

Read the recipe. Then match the two halves of the sentences.

Chocolate Brownies

Ingredients	Directions
1/2 cup butter 4 oz. chocolate 4 eggs, at room temperature 1/2 teaspoon salt 2 cups sugar 1 teaspoon vanilla 1 cup sifted flour 1 cup chopped nuts	Heat the butter and chocolate slowly until they melt. Mix the eggs and add the sugar and vanilla gradually. Add the butter and chocolate mixture to the egg mixture and stir with a spoon, not an electric mixer. Stir in the flour and the nuts. Bake for 25 minutes in a 9 x 9-inch pan. Eat the brownies the same day or wrap them in foil.

_d_ **1.** If you don't heat the butter and chocolate slowly,

_____ **2.** If you use an electric mixer,

_____ **3.** If you don't sift the flour,

_____ **4.** If you bake them for an hour,

_____ **5.** If you wrap the brownies in foil,

a. the mixture will get lumpy.

b. they will burn.

c. they will stay fresh for several days.

d. the butter will burn.

e. the mixture will get too smooth.

Your Turn

What cooking tips do you know? Think of something you know how to cook or use an idea from the list.

Example:
If you put a boiled egg in cold water, it will be easier to peel.

boiling eggs
keeping bread fresh
preventing crying when chopping an onion
making rice
making coffee or tea

14b Unreal Conditional Sentences in the Present or Future

Form

What **would** you **do** if you **saw** someone breaking into your house?

A sentence that expresses an unreal condition in the present or future has a past tense verb in the *if* clause, and *would* or *could* + a base verb in the main clause.

IF CLAUSE			MAIN CLAUSE		
Subject	Past Tense Verb		Subject	*Would/Could* + Base Verb	
If I	**had**	a problem,	I	**would tell**	you.
If we	**were**	on vacation,	we	**would be**	on the beach.
If she	**weren't***	so busy,	she	**could help**	you.
If I	**were***	you,	I	**wouldn't accept**	that offer.

*Careful speakers usually use *were* when the subject is *I, he, she, it,* or a singular noun. However, many people use *was*. In academic and formal business situations, it's better to use *were*.

1. We use *if* + simple past in the *if* clause and *would/could* + base verb in the main clause to talk about an unreal, hypothetical, or contrary-to-fact situation in the present or future.

> If you **got up** earlier, you **wouldn't be** late for work every morning. (But you do not get up earlier.)
> If I **had** a lot of money, I**'d travel** around the world. (But I don't have a lot of money.)

2. We often use *were* as a way of giving advice. The *if* clause with *were* makes the sentence sound softer.

> A: Do you think that I can turn my paper in a few days late?
> B: If I **were** you, I**'d ask** the instructor.

3. We can use *could* instead of *would* in the main clause. *Could* means *would be able to*.

> If I **had** more time, I **could help** you.
> If I **had** a computer, I **could send** you email tomorrow.

4. Practice

Write what you would and wouldn't do in each situation. Give a reason for your advice.

1. If you found a wallet with $500 in it in a taxi, what would you do? Why?

   If I found a wallet with $500 in it, I would give it to the driver.
   Maybe the person who lost it would call the taxi company.
   If I found a wallet with $500 in it, I wouldn't keep it.
   I don't think that's honest.

2. If a burglar broke into your house at night, and you were alone, what would you do? Why?

   _____
   _____
   _____
   _____
   _____

3. If you saw someone stealing some cans of soup in the supermarket, what would you do? Why?

_____

_____

_____

_____

_____

4. If a car hit a cyclist, the driver didn't stop, and the cyclist was left lying injured in the road, what would you do? Why?

_____

_____

_____

_____

_____

5 | Your Turn

Think of a situation where you had to make a difficult decision. Describe the situation to a partner. Your partner will try to imagine what he or she would do in that same situation.

Example:
Once the clerk at the supermarket gave me $20 too much in change. I noticed it, but I didn't say anything. I just kept the money. I still feel bad about it.
What would you do in that situation?

14c Unreal Conditional Sentences in the Past; Mixed Conditional Sentences

If we **had left** earlier, we **wouldn't be** in this traffic.

UNREAL CONDITIONAL SENTENCES IN THE PAST

IF CLAUSE			MAIN CLAUSE		
Subject	Past Perfect Verb		Subject	*Would/Could* + Base Verb	
If I	**had worked**	harder,	I	**would have done**	better.
If Isis	**hadn't been**	so busy,	she	**might have helped**	you.
If we	**hadn't helped**	the man,	he	**could have died.**	.

MIXED CONDITIONAL SENTENCES

IF CLAUSE			MAIN CLAUSE		
Subject	Verb		Subject	Verb	
If we	**had left**	earlier,	we	**would be**	home now.
If Dad	**had given**	me the car,	we	**could drive**	to the beach.
If they	**hadn't broken**	the DVD,	they	**could be watching**	a movie now.
If I	**were**	you,	I	**would have**	walked.

UNREAL CONDITIONAL SENTENCES IN THE PAST

1. We use the past unreal conditional to talk about an unreal, hypothetical, or contrary-to-fact situation in the past. Both clauses refer to unreal conditions in the past.

> If she **had had** the opportunity, she **would have gone** to college.
> (But she didn't have the opportunity, and she didn't go to college.)

> If you **had seen** the movie, you **would have enjoyed** it.
> (But you didn't see the movie, so you didn't have the opportunity to enjoy it.)

> If it **hadn't rained** all morning, we **would have gone out**.
> (But it did rain all morning, and we didn't go out.)

2. We can use the modals *would, might,* and *could* in the main clause.

We use *would have* + past participle in the main clause if we think the past action was certain.

> If I **had seen** you yesterday, I **would have given** the money to you then.
> (I would definitely have given it to you.)

We use *might have* + past participle in the main clause if we think the past action was possible.

> If you **had taken** the test, you **might have passed** it. (It's possible that you would have passed it.)

We use *could have* + past participle to say that someone would have been able to do something in the past.

> We **could have eaten** in the park if we **had brought** some food with us.
> (We would have been able to eat in the park.)

In some parts of the United States, people use *would have* + a past participle in the *if* clause, as well as in the main clause.

> If you would've said something, I wouldn't have bought it.

This usage is not generally considered to be grammatically correct.

MIXED CONDITIONAL SENTENCES

3. Conditional sentences can have mixed tense sequences, but the tenses must make sense in the context.

| Past Unreal Conditions. | If he **had played** basketball in high school, he **would be** a great college player now. (He didn't play football in the past, and he isn't a great college player now.) | Present Unreal Conditions. |

| Present Unreal Conditions. | If John **were** my child, I **would have encouraged** him to play basketball, not football. (John is not my child now. I didn't encourage him to play basketball.) | Past Unreal Conditions. |

6 Practice

A. Read the story of Romeo and Juliet.

Romeo and Juliet are in love, but their families hate each other. The young couple know that they will never get permission to marry, so they decide to marry secretly. A friendly friar* agrees to perform the marriage ceremony. After the ceremony, Romeo finds his friends in a fight. Romeo kills Juliet's cousin because the cousin had killed his best friend. Romeo is then sent away from the city as a punishment. Juliet's father wants Juliet to marry another man, so Juliet goes to the friar for help. He gives her a sleeping potion** to make her appear dead, and he says that he will send a message to Romeo to come and take her away. However, Romeo never receives the message. When he hears of Juliet's death, he goes to the tomb to see her dead body. In despair, he drinks poison and dies. At that moment, the friar's drink wears off, and Juliet wakes up to find Romeo dead beside her. When she realizes what has happened, Juliet takes Romeo's dagger*** and kills herself.

*Friar: a man in a Roman Catholic order
**Sleeping potion: a liquid that makes you sleep
***Dagger: a kind of knife

B. Answer the questions in complete sentences. For some questions, you must think of your own answer.

1. What would have happened if Romeo and Juliet hadn't fallen in love?

   If they hadn't fallen in love, this story wouldn't have happened.

2. What would Romeo and Juliet have done if the friar hadn't married them?

   _____

3. What would Juliet have done if the friar had not given her the sleeping potion?

   _____

4. What would Romeo have done if he had received the friar's message?

   _____

5. What would have happened if Romeo had not taken the poison?

   _____

6. What would have happened if Juliet had not killed herself?

   _____

C. Complete the sentences about the story. Use *might have* or *could have* in your answers.

1. If Romeo had not met Juliet, he *might have married someone else.*

   _____

2. If Romeo and Juliet's families had not hated each other, _____

   _____

3. If Romeo's friends had not been in a fight, _____

   _____

4. If Juliet had not taken the sleeping potion, _____

   _____

5. If Juliet had not found Romeo's dagger, _____

   _____

6. If Juliet had woken up a little sooner, _____

   _____

D. What would you have done if you were Romeo? If you were Juliet?

1. If I were Juliet, I would have _____

_____

2. If I were Romeo, I would have _____

_____

3. If I were the friar, I would have _____

_____

4. If I were Juliet's father, I would have _____

_____

---

7 | **Your Turn**

Think of a past event in your life that could have been very different. Write three sentences about what would or would not have happened in your life if the event had been different.

Example:
If I hadn't graduated from high school, I wouldn't have gotten into college.

14d Conditional Sentences with *As If* and *As Though*

Form / Function

Tim: It looks **as if** someone has a sense of humor.
Sue: It also looks **as if** someone can't spell.

1. We use *as if* before a subject and a verb to say how someone or something seems. We can use *as though* instead of *as if*.

When *as if* or *as though* are followed by the simple present or *will/be going to,* the situation might be real.

> He looks **as if** he's cold. OR He looks **as though** he's cold.
> (He looks cold, but I don't know if he really is cold.)
> It looks **as if** it's going to snow. OR It looks **as though** it's going to snow.
> (The weather looks like it might snow, but I don't know if it really will snow.)

2. When we use *as if* or *as though* + a past tense verb to talk about the present, the situation is unreal or probably unreal.

> He's acting **as if** he **were** my father. (He definitely is not my father.)
> I felt **as though** I **had run** a marathon. (I definitely did not run a marathon.)

Careful speakers use *were* instead of *was* in unreal situations.

3. In informal English, we often use *like* instead of *as if* or *as though.* However, we use *as if* and *as though* in formal writing.

> He looks **like** he's cold.
> It looks **like** it's going to snow.

---

8 Practice

Read the descriptions. What do you think is going to happen? Use *as if, as though,* and *like.*

1. There are big black clouds in the sky.

  It looks as if it is going to rain.

2. Stan has a headache and a sore throat, and he keeps sneezing.

  He feels _____

3. My neighbors are shouting, and I can hear dishes breaking.

  It sounds _____

4. My brother applied for a new job, and they invited him to go for an interview in Seoul.

  It looks _____

5. My friend has just finished her exam, and she is smiling confidently.

  She looks _____

6. There is a lot of cheering and clapping coming from the office next door.

  It sounds _____

7. The classroom is empty. The tables are covered with paper plates and cups and pieces of leftover sandwiches.

It looks _____

8. Ron looked very unhappy this morning, and I heard him crying earlier.

It sounds _____

---

9 **Your Turn**

Look at the photo.
What do you think has happened?
What do you think is going to happen?

14e Conditional Sentences Without *If*

Form / Function

Had we **known** it would rain so
much, we would have stayed home.

1. We can sometimes omit *if* and invert the auxiliaries *had, were,* or *should* and the subject in the *if* clause. This form is more common with *had* than with *were* or *should*.

If I had known you were coming, I would have prepared some food.
Had I known you were coming, I would have prepared some food.

If I were you, I wouldn't go.
Were I you, I wouldn't go.

If I should see him, I'll give him the message.
Should I see him, I'll give him the message.

Careful speakers use *were* instead of *was* in unreal situations.

2. We can sometimes imply (not say something directly) a real or unreal conditional. We use other words and phrases such as *if so*, *if not*, *otherwise*, *with*, or *without*.

	Implied Conditional	Conditional
otherwise	I didn't hear the phone; otherwise, I would have answered it.	If I had heard the phone, I would have answered it.
if so	This sounds like a good opportunity. If so, you should take it.	If you think it is a good opportunity, you should take it.
if not	I think that the earliest flight is at 8:00 A.M. If not, wait for the next one.	If the earliest flight is not at 8:00 A.M., wait for the next one.
without	Without your help, I couldn't have done this.	If you hadn't helped me, I couldn't have done this.
with	With your help, I will be able to do this.	If you help me, I will be able to do this.

10 Practice

A. Read Ms. Winters's letter of complaint about a product that she has bought.

Dear Mr. McMullen:

I am writing to complain about a kitchen mixer that I purchased in your store in December. It was a birthday present for my mother. The first time we tried to use it, it splashed tomato soup all over the kitchen walls!

(1) Had I known the mixer was faulty, I would never have bought it. **(2)** I'm sure that we would have enjoyed her birthday better without buying your mixer. **(3)** Had your mixer not been faulty, we would not have spent two hours that morning cleaning up the mess.

I would like a complete refund and some compensation for the damage to my kitchen. **(4)** Otherwise, I will take the matter to my lawyer. **(5)** Were our home not so far away, I would bring the mixer back personally.

(6) Should I need any kitchen appliances in the future, you can be sure I will not purchase them at your store!

Yours sincerely,

Susan Winters

Susan Winters

B. Rewrite the numbered sentences from the letter in 11A as conditional sentences using *if*.

1. *If I had known that the mixer was faulty, I would never have bought it.*

2. _____

    _____

3. _____

    _____

4. _____

    _____

5. _____

    _____

6. _____

    _____

11 What Do You Think?

Is Ms. Winters's letter of complaint an effective one? Why or why not?

12 Practice

A. Read the store's response to Ms. Winters.

Best Buy Appliances
1105 N. 6th St.
Tulsa, OK 74821

December 20, 20XX

Dear Ms. Winters:

I am writing to apologize for the faulty mixer that you purchased from our store in December.

(1) If we had known the mixer was faulty, we would never have sold this model in our store. **(2)** The sales assistant would have identified the fault if he had tried out the machine before selling it to you. **(3)** If we had not received this information from you, we would have continued selling faulty mixers to other customers. **(4)** If you wish to have a replacement mixer, we will send one out to you immediately. **(5)** If you do not wish to have a replacement, we can offer you a complete refund.

---

(6) If you were to have any further problems with the replacement mixer, please let us know immediately. (7) If you have any other questions, please do not hesitate to get in touch.

We hope you are satisfied with our service. Please shop with us again in the future.

Yours sincerely,

Andrew McMullen

Andrew McMullen
Customer Service Manager

B. Rewrite the sentences in 13A as conditional clauses without *if*. Start your sentences with words from the list.

had he   had we   should you   should you   were you   without

1. *Had we known that the mixer was faulty, we would never have sold this model in our store.*

2. _____

3. _____

4. _____

5. _____

6. _____

7. _____

13 Your Turn

Work with a partner. Write three past conditional sentences with *if*. Give them to your partner. Your partner will rewrite them as sentences without *if*.

Example:
If I'd known about downloading songs from the Internet for a dollar, I wouldn't have bought so many CDs.
Had I known . . .

14f Wishes About the Present, Future, and Past; *Hope*

I **wish** I **had chosen** another day for the picnic.

WISHES ABOUT THE PRESENT AND FUTURE

MAIN CLAUSE			NOUN CLAUSE		
Subject	*Wish*	*(That)*	Subject	Verb	
I	wish		I	**had**	a car.
He	wishes		he	**were**	here.
We	wish		you	**could come.**	
You	wish	(that)	she	**would stop**	complaining.
They	wish		you	**would come**	with me tomorrow.

1. For wishes referring to the present or the future, we use *wish* in the simple present + a noun clause with a simple past verb or *would/could* + a base verb.

    I **wish** you**'d come** with me.　　(I want you to come with me, but I don't think you will.)

    I **wish** I **could leave** now.　　(I can't leave now.)

2. The use of *that* in a wish clause is optional. We often omit it.

3. Careful speakers use *were* instead of *was* in unreal situations.

WISHES ABOUT THE PAST

MAIN CLAUSE			NOUN CLAUSE		
Subject	*Wish*	*(That)*	Subject	Past Perfect Tense Verb	
I	wish		I	**had gone**	with you.
He	wishes	(that)	we	**had come**	earlier.
She	wished		she	**had booked**	her flight earlier.

1. We use *wish* + the simple past or *would/could* + a base verb to say that we would like something to be different in the present and future.

   > I **wish** I **had** a car. (I do not have a car.)
   > He **wishes** he **could play** the guitar. (He cannot play the guitar.)

2. We use *would* after *wish* to express future action that we want to happen.

   > I **wish** you**'d come** with me to the doctor. I'm scared to go by myself.
   > I **wish** the situation **would change** soon.

3. We can also use *would* after *wish* when we want something to stop happening, or we want something to change, but it probably won't.

   > I **wish** she **would stop** complaining!
   > I **wish** people **wouldn't pick** the flowers.

4. We use *wish* + the past perfect tense to express regret that something happened or did not happen in the past.

   > He **wishes** he **had asked** her about it. (He did not ask her about it.)
   > I **wish** I **hadn't gone** to bed so late. (I did go to bed late.)

5. We use *wish* to express a desire for an unreal situation, but we use *hope* to express a desire for a possible real situation. Note the different tenses that follow.

   After *wish,* the simple past shows the unreal situation. After *hope,* the simple present or future shows that the situation is possible. We use the simple past to talk about hopes for the past.

   > Unreal Situation: I wish I **had** more time. (I don't have more time.)
   > Possible Situation: I hope I **have** more time. OR I hope I**'ll have** more time.
   >   (Maybe I will have more time. I hope so.)
   >
   > Unreal Situation: I wish the children **had slept** enough last night.
   >   (They didn't sleep enough.)
   > Possible Situation: I hope the children **slept** enough last night.
   >   (Maybe they slept enough. I hope so.)

14 Practice

A. For many reasons, Oscar isn't very happy. Write wishes for Oscar that will make him happy.

1. Oscar isn't rich. _He wishes he was/were rich._

2. His life isn't exciting. _____

3. His apartment is small. _____

4. He feels tired. _____

5. He doesn't have any friends. _____

6. He can't play the guitar. _____

B. Here's what happened to Oscar last week. Write Oscar's wishes after each event.

1. His car broke down. _He wishes his car hadn't broken down._

2. He ate all the food in his refrigerator. _____

3. He didn't pay his phone bill last month. _____

4. He spent all the money on his credit card. _____

5. He was late for work and got fired. _____

6. He couldn't find another job. _____

15 Your Turn

1. Write five things you wish were different about your life right now.

2. Write five things you wish you hadn't done last weekend.

Example:
I wish I didn't have to do so much homework.
I wish I hadn't spent so much time at my computer.

_____

_____

_____

_____

_____

14g Conditional Sentences with *If Only*

If only I **were** bigger.

1. *If only* has the same meaning as *wish* or *hope*, but it is more emphatic. We use *if only* in conversation and in informal writing.

2. When we use a simple present after *if only*, we hope that something may become real in the present or future.

    If only I **get** the news today. (I really hope that I get the news.)
    If only my boss **is not** in the office today! (I really hope that he won't be in the office.)

3. We use the simple past form after *if only* when we wish for something that is unreal in the present.

    If only he **trusted** me. (He doesn't trust me, and I wish he did.)
    If only I **were** ready for this test. (I'm not ready for it, and I wish I were.)
    If only we **knew** his address. (We don't know his address, but I wish we did.)

    Remember, careful speakers use *were* instead of *was* in unreal situations.

4. We use *if only* + past perfect when we wish something had happened differently in the past.

    If only I **had explained** the situation to him. (I wish I had explained the situation to him, but I didn't.)

16 | Practice

Write wishes for Linda using *if only*.

1. Linda isn't athletic.

   She thinks, "<u>*If only I were athletic.*</u>   "

2. She isn't rich.

   She thinks, "_____ "

3. She doesn't have much free time.

   "_____ "

4. She has to work very hard.

   "_____ "

5. She can't sing or dance.

   "_____ "

6. She can't drive a car.

   "_____ "

7. She doesn't have a boyfriend.

   "_____ "

8. She worries about her life all the time.

   "_____ "

17 | Your Turn

Write three regrets you have about your life. Write sentences starting with *if only*. Share with a partner. Your partner will try to guess why you regret them.

Example:
You: If only I had learned to drive!
Your partner: Is that because you wish you didn't have to take the bus every day?

REVIEW

1 Review (14a–14c, 14e–14f)

Match the parts of the sentences.

__f__	**1.** If it snows,	**a.** otherwise, I would have told you it's sweet.
_____	**2.** Had I known you were hungry,	**b.** I would put on a sweater.
_____	**3.** Without your help,	**c.** I'd go to Australia.
_____	**4.** If you need company,	**d.** leave a message.
_____	**5.** I only wish	**e.** quit right now.
_____	**6.** I didn't taste it;	**f.** we can go skiing.
_____	**7.** If I don't answer the phone,	**g.** I would have made a sandwich.
_____	**8.** If I had more vacation days,	**h.** I'll go with you.
_____	**9.** If I were cold,	**i.** I hadn't bought those shoes.
_____	**10.** I hate my job. I wish I could	**j.** I couldn't have finished this job.

2 Review (14b–14d, 14f)

Complete the sentences with *if, as if, as though, if only, even if,* or *wish.*

Jim: I'm in trouble! My boss saw me playing golf

yesterday after I called the office to say I was sick.

Now he's acting _____*as if*_____
 ₁

I were a criminal.

Kelley: _____ you had checked
 ₂

with me, I would have told you that he had

a golf game yesterday.

Jim: When I saw him, I felt _____ a truck had hit me. I

                  3

_____ you'd come with me to his office.

          4

Kelly: Oh no! _____ you gave me a million dollars, I wouldn't

              5

go into that office.

Jim: It's looks _____ things can't get worse. I _____

            6   7

I'd never called the office to say I was sick. I _____ I had a

                        8

good excuse. I _____ I could change what happened.

            9

_____ I had gone to another golf course, he would never

          10

have seen me.

Kelly: You're acting _____ your choice of golf course was what

            11

you did wrong. _____ you hadn't called to say you were

            12

sick and then gone golfing, you wouldn't be in trouble! _____

                        13

you play with fire, you get burned. _____ you took your

              14

work more seriously, you wouldn't be in trouble.

Jim: I know.

Kelly: Anyway, _____ I were you, I'd tell the truth from

          15

now on.

Jim: Yes, it looks _____ I'll have to change my ways.

            16

Kelly: You sound _____ that were a bad thing. You know that

            17

you need to change _____ you want to keep your job.

              18

Jim: I know. I know. I _____ you would stop talking about it.

            19

I've learned my lesson. But I still _____ I were rich so I

            20

wouldn't have to work at all!

Review (14a–14c, 14f)

Complete the sentences with the correct forms of the verbs in parentheses. If there are other words in parentheses, include them.

Well, I am here on vacation, and I'm miserable. I wish I (never, come)

_____*had never come*_____ to this place. It's really hot and humid. When I got off the
    1

plane, I felt as though I (walk) _____ into a steam bath.
                              2

If I had known that it rains here everyday, I (not, come) _____.
                                                            3

I wish I (research) _____ this place better. It's not the tourist
                        4

season. There's no one here and nothing to do. Did I mention the rain? If I (be)

_____ a duck, I (love) _____ it here. It
          5   6

pours. Then the sun comes out, hotter each time. If I (be) _____ a
                                                                7

flower, I (die) _____. If there were a swimming pool here,
                    8

it (not, be) _____ so bad. Did I mention the heat? If you (have)
                  9

_____ ice in your drink, it (melt) _____ in
          10   11

five minutes. Did I mention the insects? Last night I saw a beetle as big as a cat. If I

(have) _____ a camera, I would have taken a picture. But of course,
              12

I've lost my camera. Did I mention the food? I've lost five pounds already. If I (eat)

_____ too much of this food, I feel terrible. Did I mention I hate
          13

this place? I (not, bring) _____ someone here if they (be)
                                14

_____ my worst enemy. I wish I (leave) _____
          15   16

right now.

I didn't ask the travel agent about the weather here in June; otherwise, I (come)

_____ at a different time of year. I am sure you wish I (stop)
          17

_____ complaining. Well, you would be right, of course. I need to
          18

make the best of it. Nevertheless, if you (not, hear) _____ from me
                                                            19

soon, (send) _____ a rescue team!
                  20

Find the errors in verb forms and correct them.

Anita: I wish you hadn't ~~take~~ *taken* me to this party. It's boring. I wish we could ~~have left~~ *leave*

right now.

Louis: Well, I wish you stopped telling me that. I wish we go to the movies instead.

But there's nothing we can do about it now.

Anita: If only you listen to me earlier.

Louis: If only I know you would be so difficult! You're acting as if this be all my fault!

Anita: Well, without your invitation, I won't be here.

Louis: OK, OK. If more people come, we leave, all right?

Anita: Then I wish a hundred people come through that door right now.

Louis: I wish I not tell Mark that I had the night off. If only I keep it to myself.

I usually work on Fridays. The truth is that when Mark first invited me to this

party, I said no. Then I felt as though I hurt his feelings. "I know you're

working," he said. "But I sure wish you come to my party." That's when I broke

down. I wish I'm not so softhearted. If someone ask me a favor, I can't refuse.

Anita: Well, that's what makes you such a nice person. If I don't like you so much, I

won't have come.

Louis: Thanks, Anita. If I see Mark, I tell him that we need to leave. If only we have a

good excuse. If we had a reason to leave, I feel so much better.

Anita: Never mind. He's your friend. Let's stay. If we're lucky, more people come soon.

Louis: Yes, that's right. And if it were early enough, we can go see a movie. And if

you're hungry, I buy you some popcorn.

Anita: That sounds great. I wish I don't say those things to you earlier. I'm sorry.

Without your friendship, my life is not the same.

Louis: Thank you, Anita. I feel the same way. Well, it look as though we were about to

get our wish. More people are starting to arrive. Let's say goodbye to Mark.

Write a persuasive essay about a global issue. When we write a persuasive essay, we try to make the reader agree with us. To do this, we give reasons for our point of view and support them with facts. See page 260 for general writing guidelines. See page 261 for information on writing an essay.

Step 1. Choose one of the following topics or one of your own. With a partner, think of two strong reasons for or against the topic.

1. eliminating nuclear weapons

2. reducing our dependence on oil

3. protecting endangered animals

4. the use of genetically modified foods

Step 2. Think of or research facts to support your reasons.

Step 3. Write your essay.

1. Write the body of your essay. Write a paragraph for each of your two reasons. State the reasons and support them with facts.

2. Write an introduction that includes a thesis statement. Your thesis statement should state your opinion and the two reasons for it. Here is an example. The thesis statement is in bold.

> Every minute, over one hundred acres of the world's rain forests is destroyed to make land for farms and industries. The wood from the forests is made into paper, cardboard, and plywood. Rain forests cover only about two percent of the surface of the earth, but about half the world's animals and plants live in them. **If we destroy our forests, we will not only destroy many of the world's animals and plants, but we will also threaten the livelihood of many of the native people who depend on the forests.**

3. Write a conclusion that restates the thesis statement and your reasons.

4. Write a title for your essay.

Step 4. Evaluate your essay.

Checklist

_____ Did you write an introduction that contains a thesis statement and a conclusion that restates your thesis statement and reasons?

_____ Did you present facts to support your reasons in the body?

_____ If you were another person reading your essay, would you be persuaded?

Step 5. Work with a partner or a teacher to edit your essay. Check spelling, vocabulary, and grammar.

Step 6. Write your final copy.

SELF-TEST

A   **Choose the best answer, A, B, C, or D, to complete the sentence. Mark your answer by darkening the oval with the same letter.**

1. You wouldn't be so hungry if you _____ breakfast.

   A. had eaten   (A) (B) (C) (D)
   B. have been eaten
   C. would have eaten
   D. eaten

2. I'll see her at the meeting if she _____.

   A. came   (A) (B) (C) (D)
   B. come
   C. will come
   D. comes

3. I don't know what he _____ if he couldn't work there anymore.

   A. do   (A) (B) (C) (D)
   B. will do
   C. would do
   D. would have done

4. If you _____ warned us, we would have stayed at that hotel.

   A. wouldn't have   (A) (B) (C) (D)
   B. hadn't
   C. haven't
   D. didn't

5. If only I _____ his phone number, I would call him. Unfortunately, I never wrote it down.

   A. had known   (A) (B) (C) (D)
   B. know
   C. knew
   D. would have known

6. I don't know how to do this exercise. I wish I _____ the teacher about it.

   A. asked   (A) (B) (C) (D)
   B. had asked
   C. will ask
   D. would have asked

7. There are clouds in the sky. It looks _____ it is going to rain.

   A. like if   (A) (B) (C) (D)
   B. as if
   C. though
   D. though if

8. If I _____ you, I wouldn't quit your job.

   A. were   (A) (B) (C) (D)
   B. was
   C. will be
   D. had been

9. I'm really tired. I wish I _____ on vacation now.

   A. could go   (A) (B) (C) (D)
   B. can go
   C. go
   D. would have gone

10. If you _____ tired, you should rest.

   A. would be   (A) (B) (C) (D)
   B. are
   C. had been
   D. were

B Find the underlined word or phrase, A, B, C, or D, that is incorrect. Mark your answer by darkening the oval with the same letter.

1. Unless <u>I read</u> <u>the book</u>, I <u>will be</u> able
       A   B   C
    <u>to answer</u> the questions about it.
     D

         Ⓐ Ⓑ Ⓒ Ⓓ

2. I <u>could had</u> <u>finished</u> <u>if</u> I <u>had had</u>
      A   B C D
    more time.

         Ⓐ Ⓑ Ⓒ Ⓓ

3. I <u>would</u> <u>mail</u> the application now <u>if</u>
      A B   C
    I <u>am</u> you.
     D

         Ⓐ Ⓑ Ⓒ Ⓓ

4. Tina <u>wishes</u> she <u>had</u> a better job and <u>can</u>
       A   B   C
    <u>get</u> a higher salary.
     D

         Ⓐ Ⓑ Ⓒ Ⓓ

5. When should you go to New York? If you
    <u>don't</u> <u>like</u> hot weather, the best time
     A B
    <u>to go</u> <u>was</u> in May or June.
     C D

         Ⓐ Ⓑ Ⓒ Ⓓ

6. I <u>wish</u> I <u>could taken</u> guitar lessons <u>when</u>
      A   B   C
    I <u>was</u> younger.
     D

         Ⓐ Ⓑ Ⓒ Ⓓ

7. <u>If</u> you <u>will</u> <u>mix</u> oil with water, the oil <u>sits</u>
    A   B C   D
    on top.

         Ⓐ Ⓑ Ⓒ Ⓓ

8. <u>If only</u> Tom <u>told</u> us earlier, we
    A   B
    <u>wouldn't have</u> <u>gotten</u> an extra ticket
      C   D
    for him.

         Ⓐ Ⓑ Ⓒ Ⓓ

9. Where <u>you would</u> <u>go</u> <u>if</u> you <u>had</u> the
       A   B C D
    opportunity?

         Ⓐ Ⓑ Ⓒ Ⓓ

10. I <u>could have</u> gone <u>for</u> a swim <u>if</u> I <u>brought</u>
      A   B   C D
    my swimsuit with me.

         Ⓐ Ⓑ Ⓒ Ⓓ

APPENDICES

Appendix 1   Grammar Terms

Adjective
An adjective describes a noun or a pronoun.

My cat is very **intelligent**. He's **orange** and **white**.

Adverb
An adverb describes a verb, another adverb, or an adjective.

Joey speaks **slowly**. He **always** visits his father on Wednesdays.

His father cooks **extremely** well. His father is a **very** talented chef.

Article
An article comes before a noun. The definite article is *the*. The indefinite articles are *a* and *an*.

I read **an** online story and **a** magazine feature about celebrity lifestyles.

The online story was much more interesting than **the** magazine feature.

Auxiliary Verb
An auxiliary verb is found with a main verb. It is often called a "helping" verb.

Susan **can't** play in the game this weekend. **Does** Ruth play baseball?

Base Form

The base form of a verb has no tense. It has no endings (*–ed*, *–s*, or *–ing*).

> Jill didn't **see** the band. She should **see** them when they are in town.

Comparative

Comparative forms compare two things. They can compare people, places, or things.

> This orange is **sweeter than** that grapefruit.
>
> Working in a large city is **more stressful than** working in a small town.

Conjunction

A conjunction joins two or more sentences, adjectives, nouns, or prepositional phrases. Some conjunctions are *and, but,* and *or*.

> Kasey is efficient, **and** her work is excellent.
>
> Her apartment is small **but** comfortable.
>
> She works Wednesdays **and** Thursdays.

Contraction

A contraction is composed of two words put together with an apostrophe. Some letters are left out.

> Frank usually **doesn't** answer his phone. (doesn't = does + not)
>
> **He's** really busy. (he's = he + is)
>
> Does he know what time **we're** meeting? (we're = we + are)

Imperative

An imperative gives a command or directions. It uses the base form of the verb, and it does not use the word *you*.

> **Go** to the corner and **turn** left.

Modal

A modal is a type of auxiliary verb. The modal auxiliaries are *can, could, may, might, must, shall, should, will,* and *would*.

> Elizabeth **will** act the lead role in the play next week.
>
> She **couldn't** go to the party last night because she had to practice her lines.
>
> She **may** be able to go to the party this weekend.

Noun

A noun is a person, an animal, a place, or a thing.

> My **brother** and **sister-in-law** live in **Pennsylvania**. They have three **cats**.

Object

An object is the noun or pronoun that receives the action of the verb.

> Georgie sent **a gift** for Johnny's birthday.
>
> Johnny thanked **her** for the gift.

Preposition

A preposition is a small connecting word that is followed by a noun or pronoun. Some are a*t, above, after, by, before, below, for, in, of, off, on, over, to, under, up,* and *with*.

Every day, Jay drives Chris and Ally **to** school **in** the new car.

In the afternoon, he waits **for** them **at** the bus stop.

Pronoun

A pronoun takes the place of a noun.

Chris loves animals. **He** has two dogs and two cats.

His pets are very friendly. **They** like to spend time with people.

Sentence

A sentence is a group of words that has a subject and a verb. It is complete by itself.

Sentence: Brian works as a lawyer.

Not a sentence: Works as a lawyer.

Subject

A subject is the noun or pronoun that does the action in the sentence.

Trisha is from Canada.

She writes poetry about nature.

Superlative

Superlative forms compare three or more people, places, or things.

Jennifer is **the tallest** girl in the class.

She is from Paris, which is **the most romantic** city in the world.

Tense

Tense tells when the action in a sentence happens.

Simple present	–	The cat **eats** fish every morning.
Present progressive	–	He **is eating** fish now.
Simple past	–	He **ate** fish yesterday morning.
Past progressive	–	He **was eating** when the doorbell rang.
Future with *be going to*	–	He **is going to eat** fish tomorrow morning, too!
Future with *will*	–	I think that he **will eat** the same thing next week.

Verb

A verb tells the action in a sentence.

Melissa **plays** guitar in a band.

She **loves** writing new songs.

The band **has** four other members.

Appendix 2   Irregular Verbs

Base Form	Simple Past	Past Participle	Base Form	Simple Past	Past Participle
be	was, were	been	keep	kept	kept
become	became	become	know	knew	known
begin	began	begun	leave	left	left
bend	bent	bent	lend	lent	lent
bite	bit	bitten	lose	lost	lost
blow	blew	blown	make	made	made
break	broke	broken	meet	met	met
bring	brought	brought	pay	paid	paid
build	built	built	put	put	put
buy	bought	bought	read	read	read
catch	caught	caught	ride	rode	ridden
choose	chose	chosen	ring	rang	rung
come	came	come	run	ran	run
cost	cost	cost	say	said	said
cut	cut	cut	see	saw	seen
do	did	done	sell	sold	sold
draw	drew	drawn	send	sent	sent
drink	drank	drunk	shake	shook	shaken
drive	drove	driven	shut	shut	shut
eat	ate	eaten	sing	sang	sung
fall	fell	fallen	sit	sat	sat
feed	fed	fed	sleep	slept	slept
feel	felt	felt	speak	spoke	spoken
fight	fought	fought	spend	spent	spent
find	found	found	stand	stood	stood
fly	flew	flown	steal	stole	stolen
forget	forgot	forgotten	swim	swam	swum
get	got	gotten/got	take	took	taken
give	gave	given	teach	taught	taught
go	went	gone	tear	tore	torn
grow	grew	grown	tell	told	told
hang	hung	hung	think	thought	thought
have	had	had	throw	threw	thrown
hear	heard	heard	understand	understood	understood
hide	hid	hidden	wake up	woke up	woken up
hit	hit	hit	wear	wore	worn
hold	held	held	win	won	won
hurt	hurt	hurt	write	wrote	written

Appendix 3   Spelling Rules for Endings

Adding a Final –s to Nouns and Verbs

Rule	Example	-s
1. For most words, add –s without making any changes.	book bet save play	books bets saves plays
2. For words ending in a consonant + *y*, change the *y* to *i* and add –es.	study party	studies parties
3. For words ending in *ch*, *s*, *sh*, *x*, or *z*, add –es.	church class wash fix quiz	churches classes washes fixes quizzes
4. For words ending in *o*, sometimes add –es and sometimes add –s.	potato piano	potatoes pianos
5. For words ending in *f* or *lf*, change the *f* or *lf* to *v* and add –es. For words ending in *fe*, change the *f* to *v* and add –s.	loaf half life	loaves halves lives

Adding a Final *–ed*, *–er*, *–est*, and *–ing*

Rule	Example	-ed	-er	-est	-ing
1. For most words, add the ending without making any changes.	clean	cleaned	cleaner	cleanest	cleaning
2. For words ending in silent *e*, drop the *e* and add *–ed*, *–er*, or *–est*.	save like nice	saved liked	saver nicer	 nicest	saving liking
3. For words ending in a consonant + *y*, change the *y* to *i* and add the ending. Do not change or drop the *y* before adding *–ing*.	sunny happy study worry	 studied worried	sunnier happier	sunniest happiest	 studying worrying
4. For one-syllable words ending in one vowel and one consonant, double the final consonant, then add the ending. Do not double the last consonant if it is a *w, x,* or *y*.	hot run bat glow mix stay	 batted glowed mixed stayed	hotter runner batter	hottest	 running batting glowing mixing staying
5. For words of two or more syllables that end in one vowel and one consonant, double the final consonant if the final syllable is stressed.	begin refer occur permit	 referred occurred permitted	beginner		beginning referring occurring permitting
6. For words of two or more syllables that end in one vowel and one consonant, do NOT double the final consonant if the final syllable is NOT stressed.	enter happen develop	entered happened developed	developer		entering happening developing

Appendix 4 Forms of Verb Tenses

THE PRESENT TENSES

The Simple Present Tense

AFFIRMATIVE STATEMENTS		NEGATIVE STATEMENTS		
Subject	Verb or Verb + -s/-es	Subject	*Do Not/Does Not*	Base Verb
I/You/We They	**work.**	I/You/We/They	**do not** **don't**	**work.**
He/She/It	**works.**	He/She/It	**does not** **doesn't**	

YES/NO QUESTIONS			SHORT ANSWERS	
Do/Does	Subject	Base Verb	Yes,	No,
Do	I/you/we/they	**work?**	I/you/we/they **do.**	I/you/we/they **don't.**
Does	he/she/it		he/she/it **does.**	he/she/it **doesn't.**

WH- QUESTIONS				
	Subject (Wh- Word)			Verb
Wh- Word Is the Subject	**Who**			**lives** here?
	Which (computers)			**work** best?
	Wh- Word	*Do/Does*	Subject	Base Verb
Wh- Word Is Not the Subject	**What**	**do**	you	**do** on weekends?
	Where	**does**	she	**live?**
	When	**do**	the children	**go** to bed?
	How	**does**	this machine	**work?**
	Which (computers)	**do**	you	**prefer?**
	Why	**do**	I	**feel** happy?
	Who*	**do**	they	**admire?**

*In formal written English, the wh- word in this question would be *whom*.

The Present Progressive Tense

AFFIRMATIVE STATEMENTS			NEGATIVE STATEMENTS		
Subject	Am/Is/Are	Verb + -ing	Subject	Am Not/Is Not/Are Not	Verb + -ing
I	am 'm	working now.	I	am not 'm not is not	working now.
He/She/It	is 's		He/She/It	's not isn't	
			We/You	are not	
We/You/They	are 're		They	're not aren't	

YES/NO QUESTIONS			SHORT ANSWERS	
Am/Is/Are	Subject	Verb + -ing	Yes,	No,
Am	I	working?	you **are**.	you**'re not/aren't**.
Are	you		I **am**.	I**'m not**.
Is	he/she/it		he/she/it **is**.	he/she/it**'s not/isn't**.
Are	you		we **are**.	we**'re not/aren't**.
	we		you **are**.	you**'re not/aren't**.
	they		they **are**.	they**'re not/aren't**.

WH- QUESTIONS				
	Subject (Wh- Word)	Is/Are		Verb + -ing
Wh- Word Is the Subject	**Who**	is		**speaking**?
	What (events)	are		**happening**?
	Wh- Word	Am/Is/Are	Subject	Verb + -ing
Wh- Word Is Not the Subject	**What**	are	you	**doing** now?
	Where	is	he	**going**?
	When	are	the children	**going** to bed?
	How	is	your car	**running**?
	Which (movie)	are	we	**watching**?
	Why	am	I	**doing** your work?
	Who*	am	I	**driving** home?

*In formal written English, the wh- word in this question would be *whom*.

The Present Perfect Tense

AFFIRMATIVE STATEMENTS			NEGATIVE STATEMENTS		
Subject	*Have/Has*	Past Participle*	Subject	*Have Not/ Has not*	Past Participle
I/You We/They	**have** **'ve**	**worked.**	I/You We/They	**have not** **'ve not** **haven't**	**worked.**
He/She It	**has** **'s**		He/She/It	**has not** **'s not** **hasn't**	

YES/NO QUESTIONS			SHORT ANSWERS	
Have/Has	Subject	Past Participle	Yes,	No,
Have	I/you/we/they	**arrived?**	I/you/we/they **have.**	I/you/we/they **'ve not/haven't.**
Has	he/she/it		he/she/it **has.**	he/she/it **'s not/hasn't.**

WH- QUESTIONS				
	Subject (Wh- Word)		*Has*	Past Participle
Wh- Word Is the Subject	Who		**has/'s**	**finished?**
	Which (computers)		**have**	**broken** down?
	Wh- Word	Have/Has	Subject	Past Participle
Wh- Word Is Not the Subject	What	**have**	you	**decided** to do?
	Where	**has** **'s**	she	**traveled?**
	When	**have**	our teachers	**been** wrong?
	How	**have**	they	**succeeded?**
	Which (movie)	**have**	you	**chosen?**
	Why	**has** **'s**	he	**come?**
	Who*	**has** **'s**	she	**visited?**

*In formal written English, the wh- word in this question would be *whom*.

The Present Perfect Progressive Tense

AFFIRMATIVE STATEMENTS			
Subject	*Have/Has*	*Been*	Verb + *-ing*
I/You/We/They	**have** **'ve**	**been**	**working.**
He/She/It	**has** **'s**		

NEGATIVE STATEMENTS			
Subject	*Have Not/Has Not*	*Been*	Verb + *-ing*
I/You/We/They	**have not** **'ve not** **haven't**	**been**	**working.**
He/She/It	**has not** **'s not** **hasn't**		

YES/NO QUESTIONS				SHORT ANSWERS	
Have/Has	Subject	Been	Verb + *-ing*	Yes,	No,
Have	I/you/we/they	**been**	**working?**	I/you/we they **have.**	I/you/we/they**'ve** **not/haven't.**
Has	he/she/it			he/she/it **has.**	he/she/it**'s** **not/hasn't.**

WH- QUESTIONS					
	Subject (Wh- Word)	*Have/Has*		*Been*	Verb + *-ing*
Wh- Word **Is the** **Subject**	**Who**	**has**		**been**	**trying** hard?
	Which (cars)	**have**			**breaking** down a lot?
	Wh- Word	*Have/Has*	Subject	*Been*	Verb + *-ing*
Wh- Word **Is Not the** **Subject**	**What**	**have**	you	**been**	**cooking?**
	Where	**has**	she		**living?**
	When	**have**	they		**planning** to visit us?
	How (long)	**have**	we		**waiting** for him?
	Which (book)	**have**	you		**reading?**
	Why	**has**	he		**eating** so much?
	Who*	**has**	she		**dating?**

*In formal written English, the wh- word in this question would be *whom*.

THE PAST TENSES

The Simple Past Tense

AFFIRMATIVE STATEMENTS		NEGATIVE STATEMENTS		
Subject	Past Form of Verb	Subject	*Did Not*	Base Verb
I/You/We/They He/She/It	worked.	I/You/We/They He/She/It	did not didn't	work.

YES/NO QUESTIONS			SHORT ANSWERS	
Did	Subject	Base Verb	Yes,	No,
Did	I/you/we/they he/she/it	work?	I/you/we/they he/she/it did.	I/you/we/they he/she/it didn't.

WH- QUESTIONS				
	Subject (Wh- Word)			Past Form of Verb
Wh- Word Is the Subject	Who Which (students)			gave you that ring? passed the test?
	Wh- Word	*Did*	Subject	Base Verb
	What		you	decide to do?
	Where		she	go?
	When		the children	arrive?
Wh- Word Is Not the Subject	How	did	he	do that?
	Which (movie)		you	see last night?
	Why		he	come?
	Who*		she	visit?

*In formal written English, the wh- word in this question would be *whom*.

The Past Progressive Tense

AFFIRMATIVE STATEMENTS			NEGATIVE STATEMENTS		
Subject	*Was/Were*	Verb + *-ing*	Subject	*Was/Were Not*	Verb + *-ing*
I/He/She/It	was	working.	I/He/She/It	was not wasn't	working.
We/You/They	were		We/You/They	were not weren't	

YES/NO QUESTIONS			SHORT ANSWERS	
Was/Were	Subject	Verb + *-ing*	Yes,	No,
Was	I		you **were.**	you **weren't.**
Were	you		I **was.**	I **wasn't.**
Was	he/she/it	**working?**	he/she/it **was.**	he/she/it **wasn't.**
	you		we **were.**	we**'re not/weren't.**
Were	we		you **were.**	you**'re not/weren't.**
	they		they **were.**	they**'re not/weren't.**

WH- QUESTIONS				
	Subject (Wh- Word)	*Was/Were*		Verb + *-ing*
Wh- Word Is the Subject	**Who**	**was**		**speaking?**
	What (events)	**were**		**happening?**
	Wh- Word	*Was/Were*	Subject	Verb + *-ing*
	What	**were**	you	**doing** at 10:00?
	Where	**was**	he	**going?**
Wh- Word Is Not the Subject	**When**	**were**	the children	**going** to bed?
	How	**was**	your car	**running?**
	Which (movie)	**were**	we	**watching?**
	Why	**was**	she	**doing** your work?
	Who*	**was**	I	**helping?**

*In formal written English, the wh- word in this question would be *whom*.

The Past Perfect Tense

AFFIRMATIVE STATEMENTS			NEGATIVE STATEMENTS		
Subject	*Had*	Past Participle	Subject	*Had Not*	Past Participle
I/You/We/They He/She/It	**had** **'d**	**worked.**	I/You/We/They He/She/It	**had not** **'d not** **hadn't**	**worked.**

YES/NO QUESTIONS			SHORT ANSWERS	
Had	Subject	Past Participle	Yes,	No,
Had	I/you/we/they he/she/it	**arrived?**	I/you/we/they he/she/it **had.**	I/you we/they he/she/it**'d not/hadn't.**

WH- QUESTIONS				
	Subject (Wh- Word)	*Had*		Past Participle
Wh- Word Is the Subject	**Who**	**had**		**finished?**
	Which (computers)			**broken** down?
	Wh- Word	*Had*	Subject	Past Participle
Wh- Word Is Not the Subject	**What**	**had**	you	**decided** to do?
	Where		she	**traveled?**
	When		our teachers	**been** wrong?
	How		they	**succeeded?**
	Which (movie)		you	**chosen?**
	Why		he	**come?**
	Who*		she	**visited?**

*In formal written English, the wh- word in this question would be *whom*.

The Past Perfect Progressive Tense

AFFIRMATIVE STATEMENTS				NEGATIVE STATEMENTS			
Subject	*Had*	*Been*	Verb + *-ing*	Subject	*Had Not*	*Been*	Verb + *-ing*
I/You/We/They He/She/It	**had** **'d**	**been**	**working.**	I/You/We/They He/She/It	**had not** **hadn't** **'d not**	**been**	**working.**

YES/NO QUESTIONS				SHORT ANSWERS	
Had	Subject	*Been*	Verb + *-ing*	Yes,	No,
Had	I/you/we/they he/she/it	**been**	**working?**	I/you/we/they he/she/it **had.**	I/you/we/they he/she/it**'d** **not/hadn't.**

WH- QUESTIONS					
	Subject (Wh- Word)	*Had*		*Been*	Verb + *-ing*
Wh- Word Is the Subject	**Who**	**had**		**been**	**trying** hard?
	Which (cars)				**breaking** down a lot?
	Wh- Word	*Had*	Subject	*Been*	Verb + *-ing*
Wh- Word Is Not the Subject	**What**	**had**	you	**been**	**cooking?**
	Where		she		**living?**
	When		they		**planning** to visit us?
	How long		we		**waiting** for him?
	Which (book)		you		**reading?**
	Why		he		**eating** so much?
	Who*		she		**dating?**

*In formal written English, the wh- word in this question would be *whom*.

THE FUTURE TENSES

Be Going To + Base Verb

AFFIRMATIVE STATEMENTS			
Subject	*Am/Is/Are*	*Going To*	Base Verb
I	**am** **'m**	**going to**	**work.**
He/She/It	**is** **'s**		
We/You/They	**are** **'re**		

NEGATIVE STATEMENTS			
Subject	*Am Not/Is Not/Are Not*	*Going To*	Base Verb
I	**am not** **'m not**	**going to**	**work.**
He/She/It	**is not** **'s not** **isn't**		
We/You/They	**are not** **'re not** **aren't**		

YES/NO QUESTIONS				SHORT ANSWERS	
Am/Is/Are	Subject	*Going To*	Base Verb	Yes,	No,
Am	I			you **are.**	you**'re not/aren't.**
Are	you			I **am.**	I**'m not.**
Is	he/she/it	**going to**	**work?**	he/she/it **is.**	he/she/it**'s not/isn't.**
	you			we **are.**	we**'re not/aren't.**
Are	we			you **are.**	you**'re not/aren't.**
	they			they **are.**	they**'re not/aren't.**

WH- QUESTIONS					
	Subject (Wh- Word)	*Is/Are*		*Going To*	Base Verb
Wh- Word Is the Subject	**Who**	**is**		**going to**	**speak?**
	Which (musicians)	**are**			**play?**
	Wh- Word	*Am/Is/Are*	Subject	*Going To*	Base Verb
Wh- Word Is Not the Subject	**What**	**are**	you		**do** next?
	Where	**am**	I		**sleep?**
	When	**are**	the children		**go** to bed?
	How	**is**	the story	**going to**	**end?**
	Which (movie)	**are**	we		**watch?**
	Why	**is**	she		**come** late?
	Who*	**am**	I		**drive** home?

*In formal written English, the wh- word in this question would be *whom*.

Will + Base Verb

AFFIRMATIVE STATEMENTS			NEGATIVE STATEMENTS		
Subject	*Will*	Base Verb	Subject	*Will Not*	Base Verb
I			I		
He/She/It	**will** **'ll**	**work.**	He/She/It	**will not** **won't**	**work.**
We/You/They			We/You/They		

YES/NO QUESTIONS			SHORT ANSWERS	
Will	Subject	Base Verb	Yes,	No,
	I		you **will.**	you **won't.**
	you		I **will.**	I **won't.**
Will	he/she/it	**work** tomorrow?	he/she/it **will.**	he/she/it **won't.**
	you		we **will.**	we **won't.**
	we		you **will.**	you **won't.**
	they		they **will.**	they **won't.**

WH- QUESTIONS

	Subject (Wh- Word)	*Will*		Base Verb
Wh- Word Is the Subject	Who	**will**		**help** me?
	What	**'ll**		**happen** next?
	Wh- Word	*Will*	Subject	Base Verb
Wh- Word Is Not the Subject	What	**will**	you	**do** next?
	Where		I	**sleep?**
	When		the children	**go** to bed?
	How		the story	**end?**
	Which (job)		she	**choose?**
	Why		we	**be** late?
	Who*		I	**see?**

*In formal written English, the wh- word in this question would be *whom*.

The Future Progressive Tense

AFFIRMATIVE STATEMENTS				NEGATIVE STATEMENTS			
Subject	*Will*	*Be*	Base Verb + *-ing*	Subject	*Will*	*Be*	Base Verb + *-ing*
I/You He/She/It We/They	**will** **'ll**	**be**	**working.**	I/You He/She/It We/They	**will not** **won't**	**be**	**working.**

YES/NO QUESTIONS				SHORT ANSWERS	
Will	Subject	*Be*	Base Verb + *-ing*	Yes,	No,
Will	I/you he/she/it we/they	**be**	**working** tomorrow?	I/you he/she/it we/they **will.**	I/you he/she/it we/they **won't.**

WH- QUESTIONS						
	Subject (Wh- Word)	*Will*	*Be*		*Be*	Base Verb
Wh- Word Is the Subject	**Who**	**will**	**be**			**helping** me?
	What	**'ll**				**happening** next?
	Wh- Word	*Will*		Subject	*Be*	Base Verb
Wh- Word Is Not the Subject	**What**	**will**		you	**be**	**doing** next?
	Where			I		**sleeping?**
	When			the children		**going** to bed?
	How			the story		**ending?**
	Which (job)			she		**choosing?**
	Why			we		**working** late?
	Who*			I		**seeing?**

*In formal written English, the wh- word in this question would be *whom*.

The Future Perfect Tense

AFFIRMATIVE STATEMENTS				NEGATIVE STATEMENTS			
Subject	*Will*	*Have*	Past Participle	Subject	*Will Not*	*Have*	Past Participle
I/You/We/They He/She/It	**will** **'ll**	**have**	**worked**	I/You/We/They He/She/It	**will not** **won't**	**have**	**worked.**

YES/NO QUESTIONS				SHORT ANSWERS	
Will	Subject	*Have*	Past Participle	Yes,	No,
Will	I/you/we/they he/she/it	**have**	**arrived?**	I/you/we/they/ he/she/it **will** **(have).**	I/you/we/they/ he/she/it **won't** **(have).**

The use of *have* in short answers is optional.

WH- QUESTIONS				
	Subject (Wh- Word)	*Will*	*Have*	Past Participle
Wh- Word Is the Subject	**Who** **Which** (team)	**will**	**have**	**finished** by 5:00? **won** at the end of the game?

	Wh- Word	*Will*	Subject	*Have*	Past Participle
Wh- Word Is Not the Subject	**What**	**will**	you	**have**	**decided** to do?
	Where		she		**traveled?**
	When		they		**finished?**
	How		you		**completed** all of your work?
	Which (book)		he		**read?**
	Why		she		**read** that book?
	Who*		I		**visited?**

*In formal written English, the wh- word in this question would be *whom*.

The Future Perfect Progressive Tense

AFFIRMATIVE STATEMENTS				
Subject	*Will*	*Have*	*Been*	Verb + *-ing*
I/You/We/They He/She/It	**will** **'ll**	**have**	**been**	**working.**

NEGATIVE STATEMENTS				
Subject	*Will Not*	*Have*	*Been*	Verb + *-ing*
I/You/We/They He/She/It	**will not** **'ll not** **won't**	**have**	**been**	**working.**

YES/NO QUESTIONS					SHORT ANSWERS	
Will	Subject	*Have*	*Been*	Verb + *-ing*	Yes,	No,
Will	I/you/we/they he/she/it	**have**	**been**	**working?**	I/you/we/they he/she/it **will** (have).	I/you/we/they he/she/it **won't** (have).

The use of *have* in short answers is optional.

Appendix 5 Forms of Modals and Modal Phrases

MODALS

Simple Modals

AFFIRMATIVE AND NEGATIVE STATEMENTS		
Subject	Modal *(Not)*	Base Verb
I You He/She/It We They	can/cannot/can't could/could not/couldn't would/would not/wouldn't should/should not/shouldn't may/may not might/might not must/must not/mustn't	swim here.

YES/NO QUESTIONS			SHORT ANSWERS				
Modal	Subject	Base Verb	Yes,			No,	
Can Could Would Should May Must	I you he/she/it we they	swim here?	you I/we he/she/it you they	can. could. would. should. may must.		you I/we he/she/it you they	can't. couldn't. wouldn't. shouldn't. may not. mustn't.

WH– QUESTIONS				
	Subject (Wh- Word)	Modal		Base Verb
Wh- Word Is the Subject	**Who** **Which** (children)	**can**		**speak** Portuguese? **swim?**
	Wh- Word	Modal	Subject	Base Verb
Wh- Word Is Not the Subject	**What**	**can**	you	**do** to help us?
	Where	**could**	she	**go?**
	When	**would**	the children	**take** the test?
	How	**should**	he	**work?**
	Which (car)	**may**	you	**buy?**
	Why	**might**	he	**leave** early?
	Who*	**must**	they	**pay?**

*In formal written English, the wh- word in this question would be *whom*.

Progressive Modals

AFFIRMATIVE AND NEGATIVE STATEMENTS			
Subject	Modal	*Be*	Verb + *-ing*
I You He/She/It We They	can/cannot/can't could/could not/couldn't would/would not/wouldn't should/should not/shouldn't may/may not might/might not must/must not/mustn't	be	working at 9:00 tonight.

YES/NO QUESTIONS			SHORT ANSWERS			
Modal	Subject	*Be* + *-ing* Verb	Yes,		No,	
Can **Could** **Would** **Should** **Must**	I you he/she/it we they	be working at 9:00 tonight?	you I/we he/she/it you they	**can.** **could.** **would.** **should.** **must.**	you I/we he/she/it you they	**can't.** **couldn't.** **wouldn't.** **shouldn't.** **must.**

WH- QUESTIONS				
	Subject (Wh- Word)	Modal		*Be* + Verb *-ing*
Wh- Word Is the Subject	**Who** **Which** (children)	**could**		**be speaking** Greek? **be studying** now?
	Wh- Word	Modal	Subject	*Be* + Verb + *-ing*
Wh- Word Is Not the Subject	**What** **Where** **When** **How** **Which** (students) **Why** **Who***	**can** **could** **would** **should** **may** **might** **must**	you she the children he you he they	**be doing** to help us? **be going?** **be taking** the test? **be working?** **be talking** to? **be leaving** early? **be driving** home?

*In formal written English, the wh- word in this question would be *whom*.

Prerfect Modals

AFFIRMATIVE AND NEGATIVE STATEMENTS			
Subject	Modal	*Have*	Past Participle
I You He/She/It We They	cannot/can't* could/could not/couldn't would/would not/wouldn't should/should not/shouldn't may/may not might/might not must/must not/mustn't	have	arrived by noon.

*We rarely use *can* in the perfect modal form in statements.

YES/NO QUESTIONS			SHORT ANSWERS			
Modal	Subject	*Have* + Past Participle	Yes,		No,	
Can Could Would Should Must	I you he/she/it we they	have arrived by noon?	you I/we he/she/it you they	can (have). could (have). would (have). should (have). may (have).	you I/we he/she/it you they	can't (have). couldn't (have). wouldn't (have). shouldn't (have). mustn't (have).

The use of *have* in short answers is optional.

WH– QUESTIONS				
	Subject (Wh- Word)	Modal		*Have* + Past Participle
Wh- Word Is the Subject	Who Which (children)	could		have written the letter? have finished their work?
	Wh- Word	Modal	Subject	*Have* + Past Participle
Wh- Word Is Not the Subject	What Where When How (hard) Which (teacher) Why Who*	can could would should must	you she the children he you he they	have done to help us? have gone? have taken the test? have worked? have talked to? have left early? have visited?

*In formal written English, the wh- word would be *whom*.

Perfect Progressive Modals

AFFIRMATIVE AND NEGATIVE STATEMENTS			
Subject	Modal	*Have Been*	Verb + *-ing*
I You He/She/It We They	cannot/can't* could/could not/couldn't would/would not/wouldn't should/should not/shouldn't may/may not might/might not must/must not/mustn't	have been	working at that time.

*We rarely use *can* in the perfect progressive modal form in affirmative statements, but we do use *can't* in this form.

YES/NO QUESTIONS			SHORT ANSWERS			
Modal	Subject	*Have + Been + -ing* Verb	Yes,		No,	
Can Could Would Should Must	I you he/she/it we they	have been working by then?	you I/we he/she/it you they	can (have). could (have). would (have). should (have). may (have).	you I/we he/she/it you they	can't (have). couldn't (have). wouldn't (have). shouldn't (have). mustn't (have).

The use of *have* in short answers is optional.

WH– QUESTIONS				
	Subject (Wh- Word)	Modal		*Have + Been* Verb + *-ing*
Wh- Word Is the Subject	Who Which (children)	could		have been working here? have been watching TV?
	Wh- Word	Modal	Subject	*Have + Been* Verb + *-ing*
Wh- Word Is Not the Subject	What	can could would should must	you	have been listening to?
	Where		she	have been going?
	When		the children	have been taking the test?
	How (hard)		he	have been working?
	Which (teacher)		you	have been talking to?
	Why		he	have been leaving early?
	Who*		they	have been visiting?

*In formal written English, the wh- word in this question would be *whom*.

MODAL PHRASES

Be Able To, Be Supposed To, and *Be Allowed To*

PRESENT AFFIRMATIVE AND NEGATIVE STATEMENTS			
Subject	*Am/Is/Are (Not)*	Modal Phrase	Base Verb
I	**am/'m (not)**		
You	**are/'re (not)**	**able to**	
He/She	**is/'s (not)**	**supposed to**	**leave** early.
We		**allowed to**	
They	**are/'re (not)**		

PRESENT YES/NO QUESTIONS				SHORT ANSWERS		
Am/Is/Are	Subject	Modal Phrase	Base Verb	Yes,	No,	
Am	I			you **are.**	you**'re not/aren't.**	
Are	you	**able to**	**leave** early?	I **am.**	I**'m not.**	
				we **are.**	we**'re not/aren't.**	
Is	he/she	**supposed to**		he/she **is.**	he/she**'s not/isn't.**	
Are	we	**allowed to**		you **are.**	you**'re not/aren't.**	
Are	they			they **are.**	they**'re not/aren't.**	

PRESENT WH– QUESTIONS					
	Subject (Wh-Word)	*Is/Are*	Modal Phrase	Base Verb	
Wh- Word Is the Subject	**Who**	**is**	**able to** **supposed to** **allowed to**	**leave** early?	
	Which (workers)	**are**			
	Wh- Word	*Am/Is/Are*	Subject	Modal Phrase	Base Verb
Wh- Word Is Not the Subject	**What**	**are**	you		**do?**
	Where	**is**	she		**swim?**
	When	**are**	the students	**able to**	**relax?**
	How (much)	**am**	I	**supposed to**	**earn?**
	Which (ones)	**are**	they	**allowed to**	**take?**
	Why	**is**	he		**leave** early?
	Who*	**are**	they		**visit?**

*In formal written English, the wh- word would be *whom*.

PAST AFFIRMATIVE AND NEGATIVE STATEMENTS			
Subject	*Was/Were (Not)*	Modal Phrase	Base Verb
I	was/was not/wasn't		
You	were/were not/weren't	able to	
He/She/It	was/was not/wasn't	supposed to	leave early.
We	were/were not/weren't	allowed to	
They	were/were not/weren't		

PAST YES/NO QUESTIONS				SHORT ANSWERS			
Was/Were	Subject	Modal Phrase	Base Verb	Yes,		No,	
Was	I			you	were.	you	weren't.
Were	you	able to		I	was.	I	wasn't.
		supposed to	leave early?	we	were.	we	weren't.
Was	he/she	allowed to		he/she	was.	he/she	wasn't.
Were	we			you	were.	you	weren't.
Were	they			they	were.	they	weren't.

PAST WH- QUESTIONS				
	Subject (Wh- Word)	*Was/Were*	Modal Phrase	Base Verb
Wh- Word Is the Subject	Who	was	able to	leave early?
	Which men	were	supposed to allowed to	
	Wh- Word	*Was/Were*	Subject	Modal Phrase	Base Verb
Wh- Word Is Not the Subject	What	were	you		do?
	Where	was	she		swim?
	When	were	the students	able to	relax?
	How (much)	was	I	supposed to	spend?
	Which (ones)	were	they	allowed to	take?
	Why	was	he		leave early?
	Who*	were	they		visit?

*In formal written English, the wh- word would be *whom*.

FUTURE AFFIRMATIVE AND NEGATIVE STATEMENTS			
Subject	*Will (Not)*	*Be* + Modal Phrase	Base Verb
I/You/We/They He/She/It	**will** **'ll** **will not** **won't**	**be able to** **be supposed to** **be allowed to**	**leave** early.

FUTURE YES/NO QUESTIONS				SHORT ANSWERS	
Will	Subject	*Be* + Modal Phrase	Base Verb	Yes,	No,
Will	I	**be able to** **be supposed to** **be allowed to**	**leave** early?	you **will.**	you **won't.**
	you			I/we **will.**	I **won't.**
	he/she			he/she **will.**	he/she **won't.**
	we			you **will.**	you **won't.**
	they			they **will.**	they **won't.**

FUTURE WH- QUESTIONS				
	Subject (Wh- Word)	*Will*	*Be* + Modal Phrase	Base Verb
Wh- Word Is the Subject	**Who** **Which** (men)	**will**	**be able to** **be supposed to** **be allowed to**	**leave** early?
	Wh- Word	*Will*	Subject	*Be* + Modal Phrase	Base Verb
Wh- Word Is Not the Subject	**What**	**will**	you	**be able to** **be supposed to** **be allowed to**	**do?**
	Where		she		**swim?**
	When		the students		**relax?**
	How (much)		I		**earn?**
	Which (ones)		they		**take?**
	Why		he		**leave** early?
	Who*		they		**visit?**

*In formal written English, the wh- word in this question would be *whom*.

HAVE TO

PRESENT, PAST, AND FUTURE AFFIRMATIVE STATEMENTS		
Subject	Have/Has To Had To Will Have To	Base Verb
I	**have to** **had to** **will/'ll have to**	**study.**
You	**have to** **had to** **will/'ll have to**	
He/She	**has to** **had to** **will/'ll have to**	
We	**have to** **had to** **will/'ll have to**	
They	**have to** **had to** **will/'ll have to**	

PAST, PRESENT, AND FUTURE YES/NO QUESTIONS				SHORT ANSWERS			
Do/Did/Will	Subject	Have To	Base Verb	Yes,		No,	
Do **Did** **Will**	I	**have to**	**be** early?	you you you	**do.** **did.** **will.**	you you you	**don't.** **didn't.** **won't.**
	you			I/we I/we I/we	**do.** **did.** **will.**	I/we I/we I/we	**don't.** **didn't.** **won't.**
	he/she			he/she he/she he/she	**does.** **did.** **will.**	he/she he/she he/she	**doesn't.** **didn't.** **won't.**
	we			you you you	**do.** **did.** **will.**	you you you	**don't.** **didn't.** **won't.**
	they			they they they	**do.** **did.** **will.**	they they they	**don't.** **didn't.** **won't**

PAST, PRESENT, AND FUTURE WH– QUESTIONS					
	Subject (Wh-Word)	*Have/Has To Had To Will Have To*			**Base Verb**
Wh- Word Is the Subject	**Who**	**has to/had to**			**leave?**
	Which (students)	**will have to**			**take** the test?
	Wh- Word	*Do/Did/Will*	**Subject**	*Have To*	**Base Verb**
Wh- Word Is Not the Subject	**What**	**will**	I		**do** to help you?
	Where	**does**	she		**go?**
	When	**did**	the boys		**take** the test?
	How (hard)	**does**	he	**have to**	**work?**
	Which (car)	**do**	you		**repair?**
	Why	**did**	he		**leave** early?
	Who*	**will**	they		**visit?**

*In formal written English, the wh- word in this question would be *whom*.

NOT HAVE TO

PRESENT		
Subject	*Not Have To*	**Base Verb**
I	**do not/don't have to**	
You		
He/She/It	**does not/doesn't have to**	**be** early.
We	**do not/don't have to**	
They		

PAST		
Subject	*Not Have To*	**Base Verb**
I		
You		
He/She/It	**didn't have to**	**be** early.
We		
They		

FUTURE		
Subject	*Will Not Have To*	**Base Verb**
I		
You	**will not have to**	
He/She/It	**won't have to**	**be** early.
We		
They		

Ought To and *Had Better*

AFFIRMATIVE AND NEGATIVE STATEMENTS		
Subject	Modal Phrase (+ *Not*)	Base Verb
I/You/We/They He/She/It	**ought to** **ought not to** **had better** **'d better** **had better not** **'d better not**	**go** now.

YES/NO QUESTIONS*			SHORT ANSWERS			
Verb	Subject	*Better* + Base Verb	Yes,		No,	
Had	I	**better go** now?	you	**had.**	you	**hadn't.**
	you		I/we		I/we	
	he/she		he/she		he/she	
	we		you		you	
	they		they		they	

*Yes/no questions with *ought to* are rare. Example: **Ought** we **to** help them?

WH- QUESTIONS				
	Subject (Wh- Word)	Modal		Base Verb
Wh- Word Is the Subject	**Who** **Which** (student)	**ought to** **had better**		**leave** now? **take** the test?
	Wh- Word	*Ought/Had**	Subject	*To/Better* + Base Verb
Wh- Word Is Not the Subject	**What**	**ought**	I	**to do** to help you?
	Where	**had**	she	**better go?**
	When	**had**	the children	**better take** the test?
	How	**ought**	he	**to complete** the form?
	Which (car)	**had**	they	**better repair?**
	Why	**ought**	he	**to leave** early?
	Who*	**had**	she	**better talk to?**

**In formal written English, the wh- word would be *whom*.

Appendix 6 Conjunctions

Function	Coordinating Conjunctions		Subordinating Conjunctions	Transitional Phrases
	Simple	Complex		
	To Join Two Main Clauses	*To Join Two Main Clauses or Two Sentences*	*To Join a Main Clause and a Dependent Clause*	*Used Before a Noun or a Gerund Except as Noted Below*
Addition	and	also besides furthermore in addition moreover		
Comparison	and but	also likewise similarly	as just as	like/just like not only...but also
Contrast	but yet	despite the fact that however in contrast in spite of the fact that instead nevertheless nonetheless on the other hand	although though even though whereas while	despite in spite of
Time		after that finally first, second, etc. last meanwhile next since then soon (after) then	after as/so long as as soon as before by the time once since until when while	since the first, second, etc.
Reason	for	as a result consequently therefore	as because since so...that such...that	as a result of because of due to

Function	Coordinating Conjunctions		Subordinating Conjunctions	Transitional Phrases
	Simple	Complex		
	To Join Two Main Clauses	*To Join Two Main Clauses or Two Sentences*	*To Join a Main Clause and a Dependent Clause*	*Used Before a Noun or a Gerund Except as Noted Below*
Purpose			so that in order that	in order to (+ base verb)
Result	so	accordingly as a consequence as a result consequently therefore		the cause of the reason for
Condition	or (else)	otherwise	even if if if only in case only if unless whether or not	

Punctuation Guidelines for Conjunctions

1. Simple Coordinating Conjunctions

Main clause + **, conjunction** + main clause**.**

Main Clause　　　　　　　　　　　**Main Clause**
We asked everyone in the office for help**, but** we had to do the job ourselves.

Many writers use *and, but,* and *yet* to begin a sentence, but some instructors do not accept this usage.

Main Clause　　　　　　　　　　　**Main Clause**
We asked everyone in the office for help**. But** we had to do the job ourselves.

2. Complex Coordinating Conjunctions

ONE SENTENCE: Main clause + **; conjunction,** + main clause.

    We didn't have enough workers**; furthermore,** we didn't have enough time.

OR

TWO SENTENCES: Main clause + **. Conjunction,** + main clause.

    We didn't have enough workers**. Furthermore,** we didn't have enough time.

3. Subordinating Conjunctions

Main clause + **conjunction** + dependent clause.

    Stan cooks his own food **because** he wants to save money**.**

OR

Conjunction + dependent clause, + main clause.

    Because he wants to save money, Stan cooks his own food**.**

4. Punctuation of Transitional Phrases

Transitional phrases can come at the beginning, in the middle, or at the end of a sentence.

BEGINNING: **Transitional phrase,** + main clause.
                    Because of the weather, we decided not to go to the beach.
MIDDLE: Start of main clause, + **transitional phrase,** + end of main clause.
                    We decided, **because of the weather,** not to go to the beach.
END: Main clause + **transitional phrase.**
                    We decided not to go to the beach **because of the weather.**

Appendix 7 Capitalization Rules

First words
1. Capitalize the first word of every sentence.
   They live in San Francisco.   **W**hat is her name?
2. Capitalize the first word of a quotation.
   She said, "**M**y name is Nancy."

Names
1. Capitalize names of people, including titles of address.
   Mr. **T**hompson   **A**lison **E**mmet   **M**ike **A**. **L**ee
2. Capitalize the word "I".
   Rose and **I** went to the market.
3. Capitalize nationalities, ethnic groups, and religions.
   Latino   **A**sian   **K**orean   **I**slam
4. Capitalize family words if they appear alone or with a name, but not if they have a possessive pronoun or article.
   He's at **A**unt Lucy's house.   vs.   He's at an **a**unt's house.

Places
1. Capitalize the names of countries, states, cities, and geographical areas.
   Tokyo   **M**exico   the **S**outh   **V**irginia
2. Capitalize the names of oceans, lakes, rivers, and mountains.
   the **P**acific **O**cean   **L**ake **O**ntario   **M**t. **E**verest
3. Capitalize the names of streets, schools, parks, and buildings.
   Central **P**ark   **M**ain **S**treet   the **E**mpire **S**tate **B**uilding
4. Don't capitalize directions if they aren't names of geographical areas.
   She lives **n**ortheast of Washington. We fly **s**outh during our flight.

Time words
1. Capitalize the names of days and months.
   Monday   **F**riday   **J**anuary   **S**eptember
2. Capitalize the names of holidays and historical events.
   Christmas   **I**ndependence **D**ay   **W**orld **W**ar I
3. Don't capitalize the names of seasons.
   spring   **s**ummer   **f**all   **w**inter

Titles

1. Capitalize the first word and all important words of titles of books, magazines, newspapers, and articles.

   The Sound and the Fury   *Time Out*   *The New York Times*

2. Capitalize the first word and all important words of titles of films, plays, radio programs, and TV shows.

   Star Wars   "Friends"   *Mid Summer Night's Dream*

3. Don't capitalize articles (*a, an, the*), conjunctions (*but, and, or*) and short prepositions (*of, with, in, on, for*) unless they are the first word of a title.

   The Story of Cats   *The Woman in the Dunes*

Appendix 8   Punctuation Rules

Period

1. Use a period at the end of a statement or command.

   I live in New York.   Open the door.

2. Use a period after most abbreviations.

   Ms.   Dr.   St.   U.S.

   Exceptions: NATO   UN   AIDS   IBM

3. Use a period after initials.

   Ms. K.L. Kim   F.C. Simmons

Question Mark

1. Use a question mark at the end of questions.

   Is he working tonight?   Where did they use to work?

2. In a direct quotation, the question mark goes before the quotation marks.

   Martha asked, "What's the name of the street?"

Exclamation Point

Use an exclamation point at the end of exclamatory sentences or phrases. They express surprise or strong emotion.

Wow!   I got an A!

Comma

1. Use a comma to separate items in a series.

   John will have juice, coffee, and tea at the party.

2. Use a comma to separate adjectives that each modify the noun alone.

   Purrmaster is a smart, friendly cat. (*smart* and *friendly* cat)

3. Use a comma before a conjunction (*and, but, or, so*) that separates two independent clauses.

   The book is very funny, and the film is funny too.

   She was tired, but she didn't want to go to sleep.

4. Don't use a comma before a conjunction that separates a sentence from an incomplete sentence.

   I worked in a bakery at night and went to class during the day.

5. Use a comma after an introductory clause or phrase.

   After we hike the first part of the trail, we are going to rest.

6. Use a comma after *yes* and *no* in answers.

   Yes, that is my book.   No, I'm not.

7. Use a comma to separate quotations from the rest of a sentence. Don't use a comma if the quotation is a question and it is in the first part of the sentence.

   The student said, "I'm finished with the homework."

   "Are you really finished?" asked the student.

Apostrophe

1. Use apostrophes in contractions.

   don't (*do not*)   it's (*it is*)   he's (*he is*)   we're (*we are*)

2. Use apostrophes to show possession.

   Anne's book (the book belongs to Anne)

Quoted Speech

1. Use quotation marks to show the exact words that someone said.

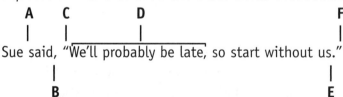

   A. Mention the speaker and use a verb like *said*.
   B. Put a comma after the verb.
   C. Open the quotation marks (").
   D. Write the quotation. Capitalize the first word.
   E. End the quotation with a period, a question mark, or an exclamation point.
   F. Close the quotation marks (").

   Here are some other ways to write quotations.

   PUT THE SPEAKER AT THE END.

   "We'll probably be late, so start without us," **Sue said.**
   (Notice the comma at the end of the quotation.)

PUT THE SPEAKER IN THE MIDDLE

"We'll probably be late," **Sue said,** "so start without us."
(Notice the commas before and after *Sue said,* and no capital letter for *so*. Also notice the two sets of quotation marks, one for each part of the quotation.)

When using this form, you must put the speaker in a natural break in the sentence.

INAPPROPRIATE BREAK: "We'll, Sue said, "be late, so start without us."

When a quotation is a question or an exclamation, put the quotation mark or the exclamation point after the quotation.

"Do you mind if we're late**?**" Sue asked.
(Use a question mark, not a comma, after the quotation, and use a period at the end, not a question mark.)
"Don't be late**!**" Sue said.
(Use an exclamation point after the quotation, not a comma.)

We can invert the speaker and the quotation verb (*say, exclaim,* etc).

Said Sue, "We'll probably be late, so start without us."
"We'll probably be late, so start without us," **said Sue.**
"We'll probably be late," **said Sue,** "so start without us."

2. Use quotation marks before and after titles of articles, songs, stories, and television shows. Periods and commas are usually placed before the end quotation marks, while question marks and exclamation points are placed after them. If the title is a question, the question mark is placed inside the quotation marks, and appropriate punctuation is placed at the end of the sentence.

Burt's favorite song is **"Show Some Emotion"** by Joan Armatrading.
He read an article called **"Motivating Your Employees."**
We read an interesting article called **"How Do You Motivate Employees?".**

Italics and Underlining
1. If you are writing on a computer, use italic type (*like this*) for books, newspapers, magazines, films, plays, and words from other languages.
   Have you ever read *Woman in the Dunes*?
   How do you say *buenos dias* in Chinese?
2. If you are writing by hand, underline the titles of books, newspapers, magazines, films, and plays.
   Have you ever read <u>Woman in the Dunes</u>?
   How do you say <u>buenos dias</u> in Chinese?

Appendix 9   Writing Basics

1. Sentence types
There are three types of sentences: declarative, interrogative, and exclamatory. Declarative sentences state facts and describe events, people, or things. We use a period at the end of these sentences. Interrogative sentences ask yes/no questions and wh- questions. We use a question mark at the end of these sentences. Exclamatory sentences express surprise or extreme emotion, such as joy or fear. We use an exclamation point at the end of these sentences.

2. Indenting
We indent the first line of a paragraph. Each paragraph expresses a new thought, and indenting helps to mark the beginning of this new thought.

3. Writing titles
The title should give the main idea of a piece of writing. It should be interesting. It goes at the top of the composition and is not a complete sentence. In a title, capitalize the first word and all of the important words.

4. Writing topic sentences
The topic sentence tells the reader the main idea of the paragraph. It is always a complete sentence with a subject and a verb. It is often the first sentence in a paragraph, but sometimes it is in another position in the paragraph.

5. Organizing ideas
Information can be organized in a paragraph in different ways. One common way is to begin with a general idea and work toward more specific information. Another way is to give the information in order of time using words like *before, after, as, when, while,* and *then.*

6. Connecting ideas
It is important to connect the ideas in a paragraph so that the paragraph has cohesion. Connectors and transitional words help make the writing clear, natural, and easy to read. Connectors and transitional words include *and, in addition, also, so, but, however, for example, such as, so ... that,* and *besides.*

7. The writing process
Success in writing generally follows these basic steps:
- ❖ Brainstorm ideas.
- ❖ Organize the ideas.
- ❖ Write a first draft of the piece.
- ❖ Evaluate and edit the piece for content and form.
- ❖ Rewrite the piece.

Appendix 10 Organizing Paragraphs and Essays

The Paragraph and the Essay

The Paragraph	The Essay
The Topic Sentence*	**The Introduction** A paragraph with general sentences leading to the thesis statement*
The Body Sentences that support the topic sentence	**The Body** Paragraphs that support the thesis statement
The Conclusion A concluding sentence	**The Conclusion** A paragraph that restates the thesis statement and adds a final thought

*The topic sentence states what the paragraph is about. The thesis statement states what the essay will prove or explain.

Sample Student Paragraph

Too Much Television is Harmful to Children

Topic Sentence   Watching too much television is harmful to children because it can take time away from studying, harm their personalities, and make them inactive. First, television takes away time from children's studies. They may not do their homework or study for tests enough. Second, their personalities can be affected by excess violence on some programs. They may get frightened or accept violence as something normal. Finally, sitting in front of the television for hours is not healthy for a child. They should be playing with friends or doing sports instead of watching the action on a screen. It is clear that, **Conclusion** watching too much television can be harmful to children, and parents should control the amount of time children watch television and the programs they watch.

Body

Sample Student Essay

Essay Organization		Paragraph Organization
Introduction *Thesis Statement*	**Too Much Television is Harmful to Children** Watching television has become a normal activity for most children in our culture today. They watch television when they are home in the morning, in the afternoon, and in the evening. There are some excellent programs for children, but many parents feel that watching too much television is not good for them. Watching too much television can be harmful to children in three ways: It can take time away from studying, it can harm their personalities, and it can make them inactive.	Topic Sentence Body Conclusion
Body	First of all, watching too much television takes time away from studying. Instead of doing their homework, children prefer to watch television. This can affect their performance at school. They may get lower grades because they haven't done their homework or prepared sufficiently for a test. They may feel tired or sleepy in class because they have stayed up to watch a late movie. They never have time to read a book, and as a result their reading skills in general are poor.	Topic Sentence Body Conclusion
	Second, some programs on television may affect their personalities. There is a lot of violence on television, especially in police stories. This may affect some children. They may get frightened and have nightmares, or they may think violence is a normal part of life and may hurt themselves or others. They often see movie stars and sports stars that look glamorous and lead glamorous lives and may want to copy them. These effects of television are not good for children's development.	Topic Sentence Body Conclusion
	Finally, sitting in front of a television set for hours every day is not healthy for children. Instead of playing with other children, and interacting with them, they become inactive. They just look at the television screen and usually eat snacks while watching television. They watch sports on television but don't play the sports themselves.	Topic Sentence Body Conclusion
Conclusion *Restatement of Thesis* *Final Thought*	In conclusion, if children watch too much television, it may affect their studies at school and their health by making them inactive and unsocial. Furthermore, if they watch the wrong kinds of programs their personalities may be affected. Therefore, parents should control the amount of time children spend in front of the television and the programs they are watching.	Topic Sentence Body Conclusion

Index